SKYTALK
English for Air Communication

GW00580169

SYMBOL LEGEND

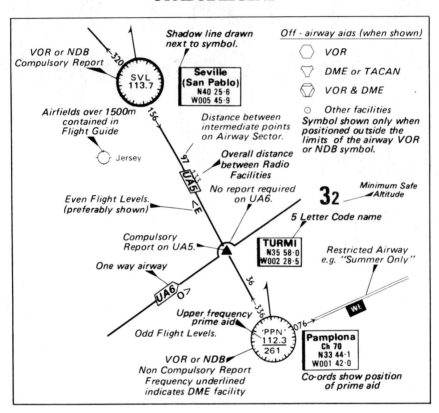

VOR or NDB
Compulsory Report

Shadow line drawn
next to symbol.

Off - airway aids (when shown)

VOR

DME or TACAN

VOR & DME

SVL
113.7

Seville
(San Pablo)
N40 25·6
W005 45·9

○ Other facilities
Symbol shown only when
positioned outside the
limits of the airway VOR
or NDB symbol.

Airfields over 1500m
contained in
Flight Guide

Jersey

Distance between
intermediate points
on Airway Sector.

Overall distance
between Radio
Facilities

No report required
on UA6.

Even Flight Levels.
(preferably shown)

3₂

Minimum Safe
Altitude

5 Letter Code name

Compulsory
Report on UA5.

One way airway

TURMI
N35 58·0
W002 28·5

Restricted Airway
e.g. "Summer Only"

WE

UA6

Upper frequency
prime aid

Odd Flight Levels.

'PPN'
112.3
261

Pamplona
Ch 70
N33 44·1
W001 42·0

VOR or NDB
Non Compulsory Report
Frequency underlined
indicates DME facility

Co-ords show position
of prime aid

S K Y T A L K
English for Air Communication

L F LEVESON

with
Martin Cass

Stanley Thornes (Publishers) Ltd

First published in 1984 by

Stanley Thornes (Publishers) Ltd
Old Station Drive
Leckhampton
CHELTENHAM GL53 0DN

British Library Cataloguing in Publication Data

Leveson, L.F.
    Skytalk : English for air communication.
    Coursebook
    1. English language — Text-books for foreign
    speakers   2. Air traffic control — Language
    I. Title   II. Cass, Martin
    428.2'4'0246291   PE1128

    ISBN 0-85950-162-0

Typeset in 12/13 Garamond by Factel Ltd, Cheltenham
Printed and bound in Great Britain at The Pitman Press, Bath

For My Mother

and

in memory of

the late Edward Bradshaw

Secretary-General of the

International Federation of Air Traffic Controllers' Associations

1978–82

CONTENTS

Unit 12

ACKNOWLEDGEMENTS

Grateful thanks go to the following people and organisations, without whose help this book would never have been written.

John Dancer (U.K.N.A.T.S.), Bernhard Ruethy and Roch Berset (Radio-Suisse S.A.), Alex Fisher, John Piper of British Airways and Captain Walter Jennes of the Dutch Airline Pilots' Association.

International Federation of Air Traffic Controllers' Associations, International Civil Aviation Organisation, National Air Traffic Service-UK, Oxford Air Training School, British Island Airways, British Embassy in Rome and Warsaw, Federal Aviation Administration of the United States, Italian Air Traffic Service, Egyptian Air Traffic Service and Polish Air Traffic Service.

The authors and publishers are grateful to the following for providing photographs and artwork and granting us permission to reproduce:

Air India (p. 106); Airports International (pp. 29, 31, 42, 44, 61, 74, 86, 95, 96, 97, 127, 129); Alia (p. 64); BAC (p. 112); British Aerospace (p. 21); British Airports Authority (pp. 25, 31); British Airways — AERAD (pp. ii, 46, 56, 57, 62, 65, 83, 85, 99, 124); British Caledonian (p. 78); Business Press International (p. 45); Chubb Fire (p. 125); Civil Aviation Authority (pp. 2, 24, 35, 51, 76, 104, 111, 113, 120); CSE Aviation (pp. 4, 11); Dan-Air (p. 17); Direccion de Aeronautica Civil, Venezuela (p. 41); Flight International (pp. 9, 51, 54, 56, 81, 82, 115, 123); Gulf Air (p. 64); Howard Harding CPR Ltd (p. 133); Japan Air Lines (p. 105); Jeppesen & Co, copyright 1984 (pp. 103, 107, 110); Susie Kornberg (p. 141); Mid East Airlines (p. 67); Pan Books Ltd, *The Flier's Handbook* (pp. 43, 98); RAF (p. 19); Selenia Industrie Elettroniche, SpA, Rome (p. 118); Shoreham and Worthing Municipal Airport (p. 22); Singapore Airlines (p. 53); Trans World Airlines (p. 52); Tunis Air (p. 60); US Department of Commerce (pp. 72, 73, 75); Usborne Publishing, *Spotter's Guide to Airliners and Airlines* (pp. 8, 122).

Note

The utmost care has been taken by the authors to follow the procedures and keep to the regulations laid down by the International Civil Aviation Organisation in the situations used in this book. It is recognised, however, that there may be local variations to these procedures, but they have not been taken into account.

Maps and charts included in this book have been simplified for use with the exercises. *They must not be used for any other purpose.*

As feet/miles and metres/kilometres are used in air traffic control in different parts of the world, both these measurements are used in this book.

INTRODUCTION

Although the use of English as the language of international air traffic control has no formal legal status, it is in fact the lingua franca of aviation communication. Generally, all communication between controllers and pilots with different mother-tongues takes place in English. (However, pilots and controllers who share a common language do often use that language to communicate.) Before pilots can fly on international routes they must satisfy the necessary authorities that they have sufficient command of English.

The problem of communication is also one of safety: accidents have occurred where misunderstanding has been a factor. The importance of air traffic controllers and pilots using standard phraseology in the international environment in order to reduce the chances of misunderstandings cannot be overemphasised. Precision of meaning is absolutely vital.

This book aims to develop the air traffic communication skills which pilots and air traffic controllers need. It can be used as part of a general upgrading of English communication, either with trainee pilots and controllers before vocational training begins, or with practising members of both professions undertaking a refresher course in English.

Those who have reached the upper elementary level in general English can easily cope with this book, and it may therefore be used alongside a general English revision book. The language in the dialogues, drills and exercises is all authentic, the text having been taken directly from 'live' recordings of air traffic control transmissions or adapted from Civil Aviation Publication 413 (*Radiotelephony Procedures and Phraseology*). All the voices on the cassette tape are those of genuine controllers and pilots and all references are to real places. The language used during radiotelephony transmissions for air traffic control has been standardised by the International Civil Aviation Organisation, and the book concentrates on this. However, certain items of non-standard phraseology are sometimes used in transmissions and these items are introduced in Appendix 1.

The emphasis in recent language teaching theory has tended to be placed on ability to express oneself adequately and appropriately in a given context, rather more than on strict grammatical accuracy. However, as already mentioned, accuracy in the use of specific terminology is at least as important in air traffic communication as general fluency, and it is important to concentrate on this in all drills and exercises. Nevertheless, those who use this book will be interested in studying English only to the extent that it helps them do their job more effectively; and to make the material more obviously relevant for them, the sequence of exercises follows the sequence of a typical flight as far as possible.

There are no formal revision exercises; however, many of the structures appear in several different contexts, so that the revision is inbuilt. The instructions for exercises and the explanations are written in very simple language, and the illustrations, diagrams and photographs are designed to be useful in teaching vocabulary and technical phrases as well as establishing the setting for the communicative activities.

As the medium of communication is radio, the language skills needed are mainly oral and aural. Since there is no face-to-face contact, the help which we usually get from facial and bodily gestures is missing; much of the material in the book is aimed at developing the listening, speaking (and thinking) skills which become doubly important in such a situation. Special emphasis is placed on learning to understand and act on instructions in English, and also to decode visual information into oral instructions or information. Many of the exercises and role-play situations are designed with this in mind.

There is very little written work, except for some short dictation exercises, which develop the comprehension skill, and some note-taking of numbers and the phonetic alphabet.

The organisation of the book

Each unit introduces the language of a particular area of air traffic communication (basic operating procedures, surface movement and take-off, distress and urgency communication procedures, and so on). The units are subdivided into a number of sections, each of which deals with a specific group of procedures used for a particular purpose.

Most sections begin with several short exchanges, or dialogues, which illustrate the essential phraseology required for the procedures dealt with in the section. Each dialogue should be listened to first for general meaning, either in a language laboratory or with a simple cassette player, without following the text in the book. Next, the new vocabulary in the glossary which follows the dialogues can be introduced. After repeating this procedure with all the remaining exchanges, they should all be played again straight through. Following this is the 'listen and repeat' stage, using the exploded dialogues, focusing the attention on the precise phraseology which is being used. Learners then listen to the unexploded version again, following the text in the book. Finally, they can practise the exchanges in pairs or in small groups where appropriate. (For fuller notes on handling the material, see the *Teaching Manual*, initially on p. 2 and then as appropriate throughout the Manual.)

The voices in the model dialogues and the listening comprehension material are a mixture of British and American speakers, so that the learner can become used to a variety of accents (some non-native speakers are also included in the 'live' recordings). It should be noted that the intonation used in air traffic communication is unusually flat and neutral (though it is still important — especially for controllers — to sound assertive and confident).

Each of the exercises which follow the dialogues consolidates understanding of the phraseology of a particular group of procedures, or provides practice in its use through manipulation exercises and role-playing. The aim is to move from the simple repetition of the dialogue stage to confident use of correct phraseology to meet the needs of a specific situation as it arises. Clearly, where learners have as yet no on-the-job experience, the role-playing stage must remain a little artificial, but it can still help to make their language learning more real, and activities involving exchanges between learners should be used as much as possible.

What this book is not

It should perhaps be emphasised that this book does not set out to teach air traffic control (or, indeed, to provide pilot training). However, one of its aims is to prepare new trainees for the specialised English they will meet in the course of their work; and if this is to mean anything, it does require some introduction to the context in which the language will be used. Practising members of the air traffic control profession have been involved in the preparation of the book, and every effort has been made to avoid *misleading* initial trainees about any aspect of the work they are hoping to take up.

If the book improves understanding of other people's transmissions in English; if it enables a prompt response in appropriate radiotelephony phraseology; and if it helps those who use it to issue instructions quickly and clearly — then it will have achieved its objective!

Unit 1

Basic Operating Procedures (1)

Numbers   Establishing Communication
Phonetic Alphabet   Time

1.1 NUMBERS

When the tape is first played, simply listen. (Notice the special pronunciation of some numbers.) When the tape is repeated, say each number after the speaker.

0	*ZERO*	6	*SIX*
1	*WUN*	7	*SEVEN*
2	*TOO*	8	*AIT*
3	*TREE*	9	*NINER*
4	*FOWER* (pronounced like *FLOWER*)	100	*WUN ZERO ZERO*
5	*FIFE*	1000	*WUN TOUSAND*

‖‖

Ex. 1   Now do the same (listen only; then listen and repeat) with these:

flight level 50	(*FIFE ZERO*)
flight level 75	(*SEVEN FIFE*)
flight level 100	(*WUN ZERO ZERO*)
heading 295	(*TOO NINER FIFE*)
1000 feet	(*WUN TOUSAND*)
1012	(*WUN ZERO WUN TOO**)
118.3	(*WUN WUN AIT DAY-SEE-MAL TREE*)

*Note 1012 is *never* said as *WUN TOUSAND WUN TOO*

Ex. 2   How do you say:

1015
runway 27
6500 feet
121.5
flight level 350
heading 180
heading 255

1

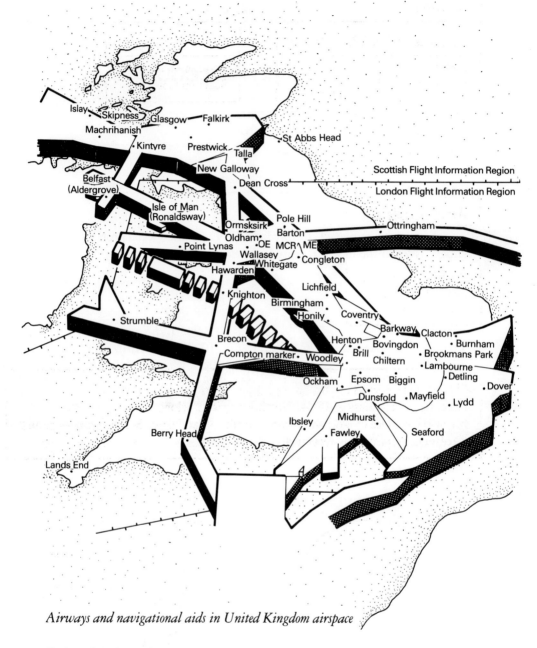

Airways and navigational aids in United Kingdom airspace

Ex. 3 **Role-play in pairs**

Imagine you are the pilot of the aircraft below. Your partner is an Air Traffic Service Unit
(ATSU). Call up an ATSU at one of the airports or control centres, giving your callsign
and flight level. The ATSU answers. Practise several times then change roles.

Example *AIRCRAFT:* *London Control Clipper 124 flight level 80*
         ATSU: *Clipper 124 go ahead*

Choose from:

Airports and ATSU callsigns	
Heathrow Gatwick Glasgow Manchester Aberdeen	Approach Tower

or

Control callsigns
London Control Scottish Control

Aircraft callsigns
Speedbird 264 Clipper 124 Air Canada 853 Japanair 405 Air India 108

flight level — see diagram on page 7
heading — compass direction (see illustrations below)
runway — piece of land where aircraft take off and land. See diagram on page 5
go ahead — pass your message

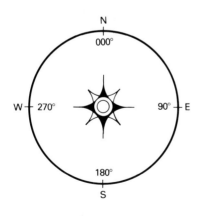

Points of the compass (true)

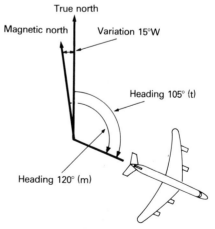

*An example of the
difference between magnetic
and true north*

1.2 ESTABLISHING COMMUNICATION

 Listen to these exchanges between a pilot and a controller. Make sure you understand all the language. Then listen to the second version of the exchanges on the tape. This time the speakers will pause; in each of these pauses, repeat what the speaker has just said. (Notice how the words are said, and copy this as closely as possible.)

Finally, in pairs, practise the exchanges without the tape. Speak clearly. (In real life, it is best to keep the microphone close to your mouth.)

1) AIRCRAFT: Heathrow Approach Speedbird 461
   APPROACH: Speedbird 461 go ahead

2) AIRCRAFT: Gatwick Tower Speedbird 711
   TOWER: Speedbird 711 go ahead

3) AIRCRAFT: Heathrow Approach Shuttle 7R flight level 90 descending to flight level 70
   APPROACH: Shuttle 7R roger

4) AIRCRAFT: London Control Swissair 256, Abbeville 47 flight level 310, estimating Biggin 10 05
   CONTROL: Swissair 256 roger

AIR TRAFFIC SERVICE UNITS	Callsigns of different ATSUs
Aerodrome Control	TOWER
Approach Control	APPROACH
Approach Control Radar Arrivals	ARRIVAL
Approach Control Radar Departures	DEPARTURE
Area Control Centre	CONTROL
Surface Movement Control	GROUND
Radar Control Service	RADAR
Flight Information Service	INFORMATION
Air–Ground Service only	RADIO

Air Traffic Controllers at work

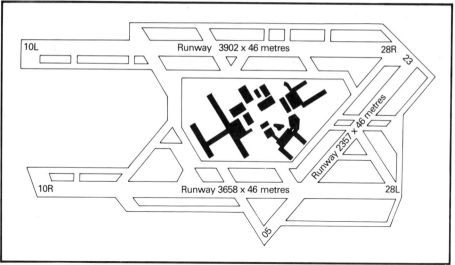

Runways at Heathrow Airport

Terms used to establish communication or to begin a two-way communication

ACFT — Aircraft

APP — Approach Control. Talks to the aircraft when it is approaching the airfield for landing (and sometimes after take-off)

TWR — Control Tower. Talks to the aircraft on take-off and landing

roger — the listener has heard the caller's message and understood it

Shuttle — a no-reservation service flying between two major cities, for example, the British Airways service from London to Edinburgh

Speedbird — British Airways callsign

flight level —

altitude —   } see diagram on page 7

height —

Biggin — a navigational beacon on the U.K. airway system, as are Willo, Holly, Fawley, Dover, Daventry and Lambourne on page 11

to estimate — say when you expect to be over a reporting point (for example, Lichfield) or arrive at an airfield

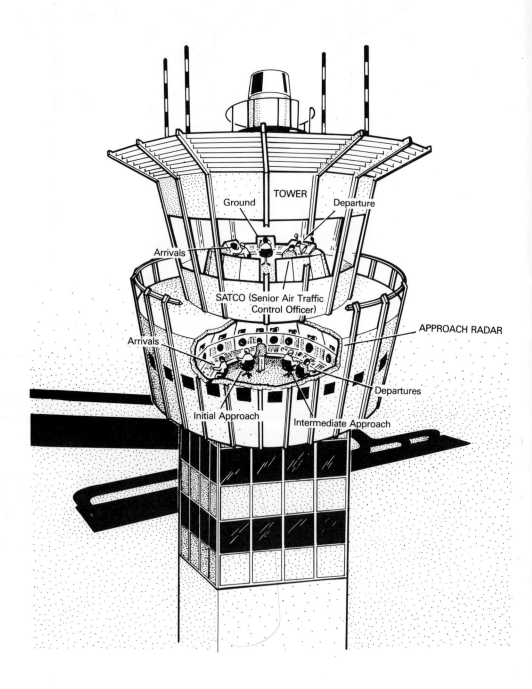

Diagram of a control tower and types of Air Traffic Service Units

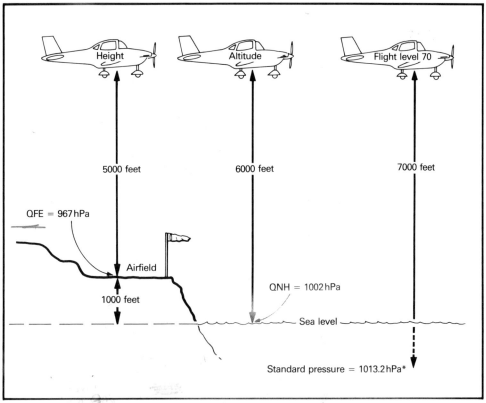

Height, altitude and flight level

The pressure at sea level (called the QNH) in the area shown in the diagram is 1002 hectopascals (hPa) or mb. The pressure at the airfield (called the QFE), 1000 feet above sea level, is 967 hPa (or mb). If the altimeters are set to these figures, they will correctly show the *altitude* above sea level, and the *height* above the airfield.

*Note that the 'standard pressure' of 1013 hPa (mb) is not a *real* pressure. It is simply a figure which *all* aircraft use, so that they know how high they are in relation to each other. (In the area and at the time shown in the diagram, a real air pressure of 1013.2 hPa (mb) would have to be somewhere under the sea — which is obviously impossible.) The same standard pressure is used at all times, everywhere in the world, whereas the QFE and QNH can vary from hour to hour and place to place.

Ex. 1 Give your callsign

When an aircraft calls a ground station the pilot always says:

1) the callsign of the station the aircraft is calling

2) the callsign of the aircraft

Example *ACFT: Gatwick Tower Air France 808*

You are the pilot of one of the aircraft pictured here. Call Heathrow Tower and give your callsign and type of aircraft.

Example *Heathrow Tower Iberia 501 DC-10*

Choose from:

callsigns		
Speedbird (British Airways)	Air UK	TWA
Clipper (Pan Am)	Lufthansa	Alitalia
Air France	Olympic	Iberia

DC-10, Concorde, TriStar, Airbus, Tupolev 154,
Boeing 727, One-Eleven, DC-3, Boeing 757, F-27, HS 748

Don't forget to add your flight number.

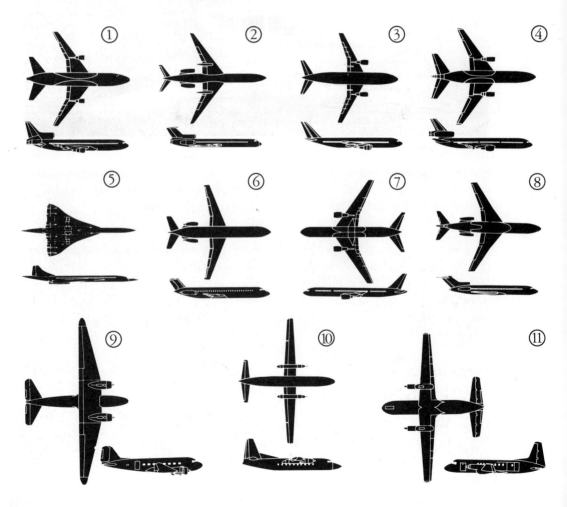

Aerospatiale Tobago

Cherokee Archer II

Jetstream 31

1.3 PHONETIC ALPHABET

 When the tape is first played, simply listen. When the tape is repeated, say each letter after the speaker.

Example *H HOH TELL*

Letters	Pronunciation	Word
A	*AL* FAH	Alfa
B	*BRAH VOH*	Bravo
C	*CHAR* LEE or *SHAR* LEE	Charlie
D	*DELL* TAH	Delta
E	*ECK* OH	Echo
F	*FOKS* TROT	Foxtrot
G	GOLF	Golf
H	HOH *TELL*	Hotel
I	*IN* DEE AH	India
J	*JEW* LEE *ETT*	Juliet
K	*KEY* LOH	Kilo
L	*LEE* MAH	Lima
M	MIKE	Mike
N	NO *VEM* BER	November
O	*OSS* CAH	Oscar
P	*PAH* PAH	Papa
Q	KEH *BECK*	Quebec
R	*ROW* ME OH	Romeo
S	SEE *AIRRAH*	Sierra
T	*TANG* GO	Tango
U	*YOU* NEE FORM or OO NEE FORM	Uniform
V	*VIK* TAH	Victor
W	*WISS* KEY	Whisky
X	*ECKS* RAY	X-ray
Y	*YANG* KEY	Yankee
Z	*ZOO* LOO	Zulu

Ex. 1   During the flight, a controller asks a pilot to report his position at certain reporting points, mostly marked by navigational beacons. The points are either named after the beacons' locations (for example, LAMBOURNE) or have separate names (for example, BEXIL). Spell these reporting points in the phonetic alphabet.

Example   HAZEL: *HOTEL ALFA ZULU ECHO LIMA*

WILLO	DOVER
HOLLY	DAVENTRY
FAWLEY	LAMBOURNE

Ex. 2   Listen to the tape and write down the letters and numbers you hear.

(Text of tape in Appendix 3)

Ex. 3   **Role-play in pairs**

You are a pilot of a light aircraft approaching Oxford Airport. Call the Tower and give your callsign. The air traffic controller (ATCO) will acknowledge your call. Use the list of callsigns below.

Example   *ACFT:*   *Oxford Tower G-BXLD*
　　　　　　ATCO: *G-BXLD go ahead*

callsigns	
G-RASC	D-ABAP
G-SJAB	F-BPJQ
C-FTJV	I-DIBD

Air Traffic Controllers at work

1.4 TIME

Listen to this

09 20	TOO ZERO
	or
	ZERO NINER TOO ZERO
16 50	FIFE ZERO
	or
	WUN SIX FIFE ZERO

Ex. 1   Say these times, then listen to the answers on the tape.

Example 20 40   *FOWER ZERO or TOO ZERO FOWER ZERO*

10 30
15 45
23 55
08 10

Ex. 2   **Practice in pairs**

Say a time (as in Exercise 1) while your partner writes it down. Practise several times then change roles.

Ex. 3   Look at the clocks below and say the times aloud:

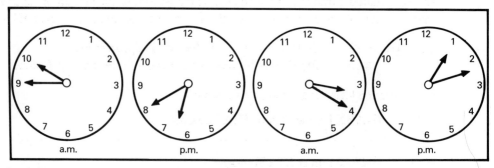

Ex. 4   Change the following times into the 24 hour clock.

Example 7 a.m.   *ZERO SEVEN HUNDRED* (07 00)
          10 45 p.m.   *TOO TOO FOWER FIFE* (22 45)

a.m.	*p.m.*
6 30	3 20
11 54	7 35
	11 50

CONSOLIDATION ——————————————————————

Ex. 1   **Report your flight level**

From the lists of callsigns and flight levels, report the flight level of your aircraft.

Example   *Air France 818 leaving flight level 80 descending to flight level 70*
Air France 818 leaving flight level 80 climbing to flight level 100

callsigns
Air France 818
Speedbird 302
Air France 963
2G-LFOB
2D-WEPX
G-BOAA (Concorde)

flight levels
70 — 100
90 — 70
75 — 65
100 — 90
60 — 50
590 — 550

Ex. 2   **Pass your message**

Work in pairs. Using the information in this unit call the station and pass your message. Give your callsign, aircraft type and position. Take it in turns with your partner.

Example   *London Control Speedbird 302 Trident over Bovingdon*

Bovingdon — see map on page 2 for names and positions of navigational aids

Ex. 3   An Approach Controller at Toulouse Airport wants to know certain information about your Estimated Time of Arrival (ETA). The positions of the aircraft are shown on the map on page 14 by large black dots. Find each position and make up an ETA.

Example   *APP: G-JMLF report ETA Toulouse and position now*
ACFT: My ETA is 50 and my position is 20 miles north of Toulouse

Complete the following dialogues in pairs:

APP: G-ABXT what is your ETA Toulouse?
ACFT: ....

APP: F-TRJF report ETA Toulouse
ACFT: ....

APP: D-GALD what is your position?
ACFT: ....

APP: G-AACX what is your ETA Toulouse?
ACFT: ....

APP: F-DTAC ETA Toulouse?
ACFT: ....

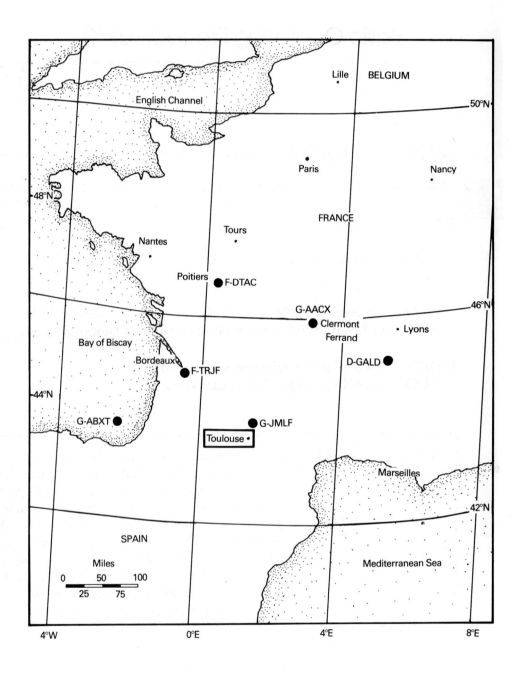

Map showing position of Toulouse Airport and aircraft for Exercise 3
Note: This map has been simplified and must not be used for any other purpose than this exercise

Unit 2

Basic Operating Procedures (2)

Abbreviation of Procedure   Readback
Correction   Transfer of Communication

2.1 ABBREVIATION (SHORTENING) OF PROCEDURE

Listen to these exchanges between a pilot and a controller. Make sure you understand all the language. Then listen to the second version. After each pause, repeat what the speaker has just said.

1) ACFT: Approach Shuttle 7R flight level 70
   APP: Shuttle 7R roger

2) ACFT: Approach G-ARPP Trident information INDIA flight level 80
   APP: G-PP maintain flight level 80. Report leaving Lambourne heading 270

3) APP: F-BNTS leave Lambourne heading 230
   ACFT: F-BNTS heading 230 from Lambourne

---

information INDIA — ATIS (Automatic Terminal Information Service) broadcasts a 24-hour information service for arriving or departing aircraft, giving the pilot information on present aerodrome and weather conditions. Every day ATIS messages begin with the letter ALPHA, and the letter changes when there is any new information. For example, 'information Alpha', 'Bravo', 'Charlie', and so on until 'Zulu'. 'Information India' tells the controller the latest message the aircraft has received.

Lambourne — a navigational beacon, to the east of London on the U.K. airway system

to maintain — to stay at same level or speed

heading 270 — magnetic heading 270 (see diagram on page 3)

Ex. 1   Listen to this example on the tape. Notice that the whole transmission can be shortened by leaving out words in brackets in the example below:

ACFT: *Stansted (Tower) G-BFBO downwind*
TWR: *G-BO report (to the Tower when you arrive on the) base (leg)*

The short form can be:

ACFT: *Stansted G-BFBO downwind*
TWR: *G-BO report base*

In the following, shorten the communications in a similar way.(DON'T shorten the *callsigns* here — you'll see why in Ex. 2.)

1) ATSU: G-AZVL (to) join (the airway) at Daventry
   ACFT: G-AZVL (is cleared) to join (the airway) at Daventry

2) ACFT: Heathrow Ground Air France 808 request push-back (from) stand 26C
   GMC: Air France 808 push-back (is) approved

3) ACFT: Dan-Air 403 (is) ready (for departure)
   TWR: Dan-Air 403 behind Viscount on (short) final, line up behind

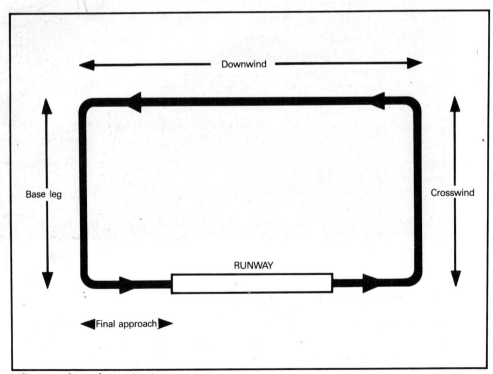

The normal aerodrome circuit

downwind — ⎱ parts of the normal aerodrome circuit (see diagram on page
base leg — ⎰ 16)

cleared — controller gives pilot permission to do something

airway — air space similar to a 'road in the sky'. The air traffic controllers direct
the traffic within these areas

apron — part of the surface area of an aerodrome

Heathrow Ground — surface movement controller at Heathrow Airport

departure — sequence of manoeuvres from the moment the aircraft leaves the
apron until after take-off

Dan-Air — callsign for Dan-Air: British airline

take-off (noun) — the moment after the aircraft leaves the ground

approved — controller gives permission

on short final — about 4 nautical miles from landing

line up — line up on runway, hold position and wait for more instructions (see
illustration of ground and departure manoeuvres, page 18)

start-up — start engines

Aircraft standing on the apron

Ex. 2   Shortening callsigns

After the first communication between the aircraft and controller (like the examples in
Unit 1), you do not always need to use certain words or phrases, for example, 'go ahead',
'roger', etc. During a two-way communication you do not need to give your full
identification every time.

Example ACFT: *Stansted Tower G-BFBO downwind (if first communication)*
         ACFT: *Stansted Tower G-BO downwind (if already in contact with Tower)*

If the registration code is the callsign, or is part of it, the registration code can be shortened (but notice that *other* callsigns, for example Air France, must be given in full):

Full callsign	Shortened callsign
G-AZVL	G-VL
N713AC	N3-AC
Speedbird G-AWZL	Speedbird ZL (training flights)
Speedbird 750	no change
Shuttle 7R	no change

IMPORTANT: aircraft only use the short form *after* the controller has used it.

Here are some registration letters (and numbers) of civil aircraft. Do you know the country they come from?

C-FCPL	F-BCYX	G-MIKE
D-AAST	HB-IST	LN-RLS
EC-ASN	HZ-AHA	N605US
EI-BAB	I-GISA	OD-AFB

Can each of these be shortened? If so, give the short form.

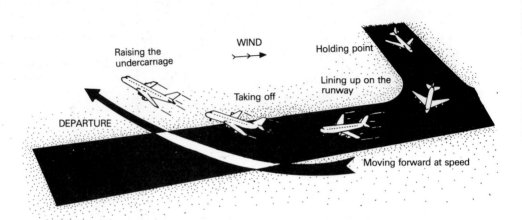

Ground and departure manoeuvres

Ex. 3 **Role-play in pairs**

You are the pilot of a light aircraft flying into Schiphol Airport, Amsterdam. Call up the Tower and report that you are on final. The Tower acknowledges you. Choose different callsigns from the box. Practise several times, then change roles.

Example   ACFT: *Schiphol Tower D-LOCB on final*
             TWR: *D-CB continue approach*
             ACFT: *D-CB*

G-ABNR	G-BOAA
G-FYOM	D-CESF
F-XJTA	N-7560V
YU-LFZ	EI-ANH

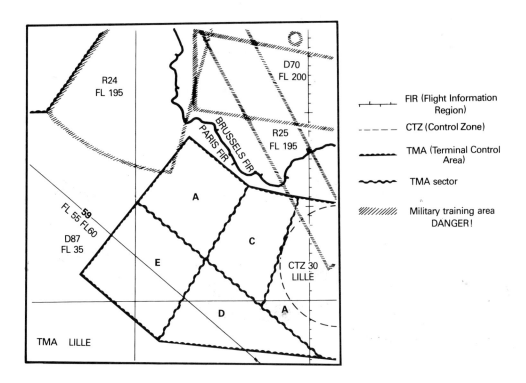

Chart showing different control areas and control zones

Ex. 4   Shorten the communications below, and either readback (repeat) or acknowledge.

Example   *ACFT: Tower Speedbird 211 I would like to request start-up*
          becomes
          ACFT: Tower Speedbird 211 request start-up
          TWR: Speedbird 211 start-up approved

1) TWR: G-BAXT you are cleared to take-off and report when you are airborne

2) ACFT: Tower G-TARD I would like to have my taxi clearance

3) TWR: G-DXLT report when you are passing the zone boundary

2.2 READBACK

Listen to this

1) APP: Lufthansa 050 24 miles from touchdown, descend to 3000 feet QNH
          1018
   ACFT: Lufthansa 050 roger descending to 3000 feet on 1018

2) TWR: G-BO hold short of runway. Aircraft on straight in approach
          runway 23
   ACFT: G-BO holding position

3) TWR: G-BO QNH 1024
   ACFT: QNH 1014 G-BO
   TWR: Negative, QNH 1024

Lufthansa — callsign for Lufthansa: West German national airline
touchdown — point of landing
straight in approach — a direct approach to a runway
QNH — altimeter setting to give aircraft *altitude* above sea level
QFE — altimeter setting to give aircraft *height* above airfield
on final approach or **on final** — the aircraft is in line with runway just before
          landing
hold short of runway — aircraft stands just before (normally 50 m) beginning of
          runway
to hold — to stop and wait or to enter a holding pattern over a beacon (see diagram
          on page 98)
negative — no
affirm — yes

Ex. 1   Always readback (repeat) ATC instructions in the same order as you receive them:

Example *APP:*   *Speedbird 726 maintain flight level 70 to Daventry*
       ACFT: *Maintaining flight level 70 to Daventry Speedbird 726*

Imagine you are the pilot of a BAe 125. Listen to the controller on the tape and readback his instructions.

(Text of tape is in Appendix 3)

BAe 125

Ex. 2   **Role-play in pairs**

Give instructions from the ATSU, choosing the correct verb. Your partner gives the readback (ACFT). Practise several times then change roles.

Example *ATSU:*   *Iberia 500 turn left, heading 230*
       ACFT: *Iberia 500 turning left heading 230*

Iberia 500	turn climb descend hold contact cross report maintain	to flight level 70 Tower 124.5 runway 23 leaving flight level 110 1000 feet left heading 230 at 45 to flight level 80 short of runway to 3000 feet QNH 1010

2.3 CORRECTION

Listen to this

1) APP: KLM 570 contact Tower on 118.4. Correction 118.5
   ACFT: 118.5 KLM 570

2) GROUND: G-XD give way to DC-10 entering taxiway 5. Correction taxiway 9
   ACFT: Giving way to DC-10 G-XD

3) GROUND: Sabena 114 vacate runway at taxiway 4. Caution, marked trench on
                right side. Correction, I say again, marked trench on left side
   ACFT: Sabena 114 vacate runway at taxiway 4. Trench on left side

---

taxiway — see layout of aerodrome below
to give way — to let another aircraft go past yours, usually on the manoeuvring
                area
to vacate — to leave
caution — pay attention — Danger!
trench — ditch
KLM — callsign for KLM: Dutch national airline
Sabena — callsign for Sabena: Belgian national airline

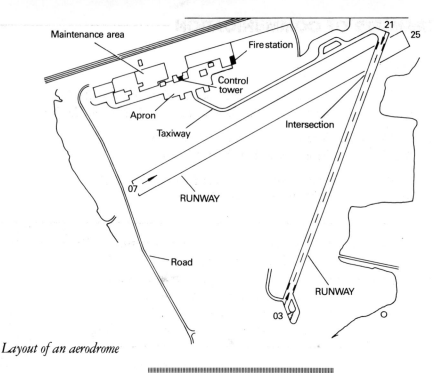

Layout of an aerodrome

Ex. 1   When you make a mistake during a transmission, say the word 'correction', then the correct version.

Example *TWR:*   *Iberia 101 give way to the B727. Correction, give way to the B707 entering the apron*
        ACFT: Giving way to B707 Iberia 101

Listen to the examples on the tape. Each time the controller makes a mistake. What is it and what is the correction? (*Text of tape in Appendix 3.*)

Ex. 2   You are a controller giving the following instructions. You make a mistake. Correct it! The correct information is in the brackets. (Give a callsign too.)

Example *KLM 330 climb to flight level 50. Correction flight level 70*

1) Climb to flight level 50 . . .	(70)
2) Descend to flight level 310 . . .	(210)
3) Maintain flight level 210 . . .	(310)
4) Turn left, heading 100 . . .	(110)
5) Descend to flight level 90 . . .	(70)
6) Behind TriStar on short final, cross runway 23 . . . (Trident)	

2.4 TRANSFER OF COMMUNICATION

Listen to this

1) TWR: Caledonian 943 contact London Control 129.6
    ACFT: Changing to London Control on 129.6 Caledonian 943

2) GROUND: Shuttle 8M monitor Tower 118.5
    ACFT: Monitoring 118.5 Shuttle 8M

3) APP: Speedbird 725 contact Arrival on 120.45
    ACFT: 120.45 Speedbird 725

London Control — London Area Traffic Control at West Drayton, near Heathrow Airport
Caledonian — callsign for British Caledonian Airways
to monitor — to listen for another communication
to contact — to call an Air Traffic Service Unit
129.6 — the radio frequency (in MHz) the ATSU is using

Sector controllers at the London Air Traffic Control Centre

Ex.1 When you change radio frequencies always name first *the unit* then *the frequency*.

Example TWR: *G-VL contact London Control on 129.6*
ACFT: *London Control 129.6 G-VL*

From the list of frequencies below, tick all the frequencies you hear on the tape.

1) London Control 135.7
2) Departure 120.4
3) Ground 121.9
4) Tower 118.4
5) Approach 124.9
6) France Control 128.17
7) Approach 119.2
8) Tower 119.7
9) London Information 124.6
10) Radar 124.35

(*Text of tape in Appendix 3*)

Ex.2 **Controller and pilot**

In pairs, using the frequencies in the list in Exercise 1, make dialogues between controller and pilot.

Example CONTROL: *Speedbird 621 contact Tower 118.4*
ACFT: *118.4 Speedbird 621*

Ex.3   **Role-play in pairs**

A light aircraft is approaching Stansted Airport (in England) from Jersey. Read this dialogue between the ATSU and the aircraft in pairs.

ACFT: Stansted Approach G-ABCT
APP: G-CT Stansted Approach maintain 2000 feet, report Lambourne
ACFT: Stansted G-CT, call you passing 2000 feet
APP: G-CT negative. Maintain 2000 feet and call when passing Lambourne
ACFT: Stansted G-CT maintaining 2000 feet call you Lambourne

(a few minutes later)

ACFT: Stansted G-CT 2000 feet and passed Lambourne 1145
APP: G-CT contact Stansted Tower 118.2
ACFT: Stansted 118.2 G-CT

Stansted Airport

Unit 3

Aerodrome Information

ATIS for Departing Flights   Essential Aerodrome Information
Weather Information   RVR Reporting

3.1 ATIS (Automatic Terminal Information Service) FOR DEPARTING FLIGHTS

ATIS broadcasts give the pilot of a departing aircraft important information about the conditions at the aerodrome, such as the surface wind, temperature, QNH and runway-in-use, and any problems, for example, maintenance work on a taxiway. The first broadcast has the letter 'ALFA' and changes to 'BRAVO' when the information changes (see Unit 2). Pilots acknowledge ATIS when they first contact ATC.

Not all aerodromes have this service. Only some major international airports have it, for example, Amsterdam, Frankfurt, Gatwick.

---

information G — since 0001 hours the information has changed seven times. The next letter will be H

magnetic — direction compared to magnetic north (see illustration on page 3). For example, 090° magnetic is the direction the wind blows from (from the east)

knots — nautical miles per hour, used to measure the speed of the wind. 1 knot = 1.15 m.p.h. (1.85 km/h)

temperature — degrees of heat, for example, −10 °C or 20 °C

dewpoint — dewpoint is the lowest temperature to which moist air can be cooled without changing to water. Below the dewpoint, dew (little drops of water) forms on the ground or in the air making fog or cloud

QNH — altimeter setting for air pressure at sea level (see diagram on page 7), for example, 1012 hPa (mb)

hPa/mb — hectopascals/millibars — used to measure air pressure (in USA, inches of mercury, for example, 29.92 inches = 1013.2 hPa)

Frankfurt Main — major international airport in West Germany

Ex. 1   Listen to this ATIS message from London Heathrow, then answer the questions.

1) What letter of the phonetic alphabet did you hear?
2) What time was the ATIS message broadcast?
3) Is that a.m. or p.m.?
4) What was the temperature of the air?
5) What was the speed and direction of the wind?
6) What was the QNH?
7) What was the number of the runway?

(Text of tape and answers in Appendix 3)

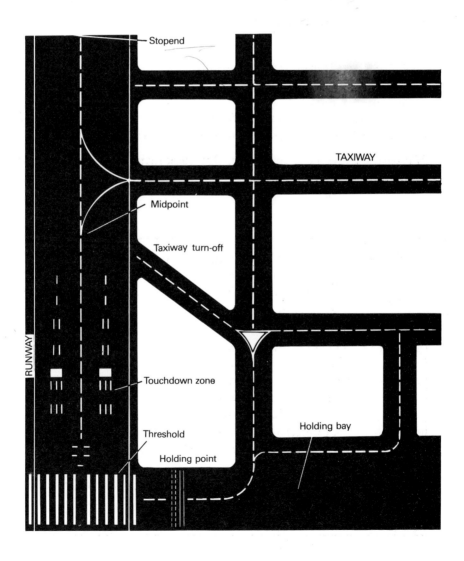

Runways and taxiways

Ex. 2   This ATIS message for departing flights is from Kastrup Airport, Copenhagen in Denmark. Listen to the tape then choose the correct answer for these questions:

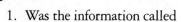

1. Was the information called
   a) X?
   b) S?
   c) C?
   d) G?

2. Was the message broadcast at
   a) 19 00?
   b) 09 30?
   c) 15 30?
   d) 19 30?

3. Was the direction of the wind
   a) 204°?
   b) 040°?
   c) 140°?
   d) 240°?

4. Was the QNH
   a) 1015 hPa?
   b) 1025 hPa?
   c) 1019 hPa?
   d) 1035 hPa?

5. The number of the runway was
   a) 32 left?
   b) 22 right?
   c) 22 left?
   d) 23 left?

(Text of tape and answers in Appendix 3)

Ex. 3   Assistant controllers record ATIS messages. Read the ATIS message below:

Frankfurt Main Departure Information M 14 00 hours   Weather
Wind 040 degrees magnetic 10 knots Temperature 06 Dewpoint
01   QNH 998 hPa
Runway in use now is 07 left

Frankfurt Airport

3.2 ESSENTIAL AERODROME INFORMATION

ATIS messages sometimes contain important information about the surface movement area or equipment of the airport which might affect the safe operation of the aircraft. However, controllers may sometimes give this information direct to the aircraft.

Listen to this

1) TWR: Yugoslav 241 taxi with caution, work in progress on taxiway 2
   ACFT: Yugoslav 241

2) TWR: KD-3351 taxi to holding point runway 08. Be advised midpoint of taxiway partly covered by ice. Braking action medium
   ACFT: Roger. Copy braking action KD-3351

3) TWR: Swissair 801 taxi to holding point runway 14. Green centreline lights on taxiway unserviceable
   ACFT: Swissair 801 roger. Taxi to holding point runway 14

---

to taxi — to move an aircraft along the ground surface
work in progress — workmen are repairing taxiway, runway or apron
be advised — Listen! Important information!
midpoint — part of taxiway or runway between the beginning and end (see illustration on page 27)
partly covered — not completely covered, for example, 30 to 40%
ice — surface covered with frozen water
braking action medium — aircraft takes longer to stop because of ice, water or snow on runway surface
braking action poor — the aircraft may not stop at all
centreline lights — they help to guide pilot along route at night or in fog
unserviceable — not working
standing water/water patches — small pools of water
vehicle — car, van, tug, etc.
shingle — small stones
snow clearance — clearing away the snow
threshold — beginning of runway (see illustration on page 27)
flock of birds — some birds
volcanic cloud — dust from volcano (for example, Mount Etna)
drifting — moving slowly
Yugoslav — callsign for JAT: Yugoslavian national airline

Snow clearance

Ex. 1   Caution!

Work in pairs. You are a controller in the Tower of a major international airport. Transmit the following information to the aircraft which is parked on the apron. Your partner acknowledges the message. Practise several times, then change roles.

Example *TWR: KLM 409 caution! Building work in progress next to taxiway 6*
             ACFT: Roger KLM 409

KLM 409 caution!	Construction work in progress on runway 21 right left side Building work in progress next to taxiway 6 Broken surface at end of runway 14 right Ice on runway 21 right, braking action poor Water patches on runway 21 right Vehicle broken down on taxiway 6 Taxiway partly covered with shingle

Work in progress next to a runway

Ex. 2   Look out!

In pairs, use the ideas in the pictures below to complete the aerodrome information the controller is giving to G-RIHM.

Example   *TWR:*   *G-RIHM taxi to holding point runway 09. Caution! Flock of birds sighted half a mile south of airfield*

             ACFT: *Roger G-RIHM*

G-RIHM	taxi to holding point runway 09. cleared for take-off.	Caution!	. . . at threshold . . . still in progress . . . marked by red flags . . . sighted half a mile south of airfield . . . reported at 5000 feet north of airfield drifting south-east and extending up to 15 000 feet

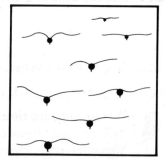

3.3 WEATHER INFORMATION

Listen to this

On the tape you will hear some examples of important weather (meteorological) information. (The text of the tape is in Appendix 3.)

FIR — Flight Information Region

SIGMET — important weather information on tape

Marseilles **FIR** — covers southern area of France (see Unit 5)

VOLMET — reports of weather conditions at major airports, broadcast twenty-four hours a day

Tunis — capital of North African state of Tunisia

Milan **FIR** — covers northern part of Italy

Naples — city in southern Italy

Tunis-Carthage — airport for Tunis

clear air turbulence — see diagram on page 34

moderate to severe — strong to very strong

sand-storm — sand blowing from the desert

earth tremor — movement of the ground

windshear — sudden change in wind speed and direction (see diagram on page 34)

severe icing — very bad ice forming on aircraft (increases weight of aircraft)

cumulo-nimbus clouds (CB) — thunder clouds (see diagram on page 34)

Ex. 1   **Listening comprehension**

Listen to the tape again, then answer these questions.

1. a) Was the message timed at 13 00 hours or 14 00 hours?
   b) Was clear air turbulence reported or windshear?
   c) Was it moderate or severe?

2. a) Was the sand-storm north or south of Tunis?
   b) Was it up to 1000 feet or 10 000 feet?
   c) Is the airport open or closed now?

3. a) Is Milan or Naples Airport closed?
   b) Were there earth tremors or an earthquake?

4. Was windshear reported at 500 or 5000 feet?

(Text of tape and answers in Appendix 3)

Ex. 2   Role-play in pairs

You are the pilot of a BAC One-Eleven. Report one of the following to the Tower.

flock of birds	braking action
clear air turbulence at flight level 300	severe icing
windshear	cumulo-nimbus clouds

Example   *ACFT: Tower Speedbird 311 severe icing at flight level 50*
         TWR: Roger Speedbird 311

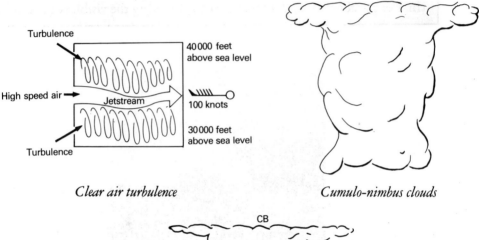

Clear air turbulence   *Cumulo-nimbus clouds*

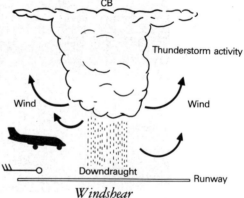

Windshear

3.4 RVR REPORTING
(Instrumented and Human Observation Method)

RVR (Runway Visual Range) is the distance visible along the runway. At major airports automatic equipment measures the RVR, but at smaller aerodromes an observer reports the RVR from an observation point at the threshold of the runway. Controllers and pilots of aircraft can also add information to the RVR report. These reports are only given when the visibility is less than a certain distance.

The different parts of a runway are shown in the illustration on page 27. The names of the parts are:

touchdown   point where aircraft land, for example, 1500 feet from threshold for a 747

midpoint   middle of runway

stopend   end of runway

---

visibility — distance at which the pilot can clearly see objects, for example, more than 10 km is very good visibility

missing — information not available

thicker patches — fog is denser in parts, reducing the visibility even more

---

RVR measuring equipment

Listen to this

These are some examples of RVR which you may hear on an ATIS or VOLMET broadcast. (*Text of tape in Appendix 3.*)

Ex. 1   **Listening comprehension**

Listen to the tape again then try to answer these questions.

1) On runway 26 right the RVR was
  a) touchdown 800, midpoint 700, stopend 600.
  b) touchdown 1800, midpoint 1600, stopend 1200.
  c) touchdown 600, midpoint 800, stopend 700.
  d) touchdown 600, midpoint 800, stopend 600.

2) On runway 26 left the RVR was
  a) greater than 10 metres.
  b) greater than 100 metres.
  c) greater than 1000 metres.
  d) greater than 1100 metres.

3) On runway 08 right the RVR was
  a) less than 1100 metres.
  b) less than 100 metres.
  c) less than 1000 metres.
  d) less than 10 metres.

Ex. 2   You are a controller at an airfield. Transmit the following RVR information.

TWR:	RVR	less than 800 metres runway 08 — touchdown 850, midpoint 700, stopend 900 metres greater than 1100 metres runway 10 right — touchdown 900, midpoint 650, stopend missing runway 28 — 1000 metres less than 100 metres

Unit 4

Surface Movement and Take-off

Pre-flight Radio Checks   ATC Clearances   Start-up and Push-back Clearance
Taxi and Holding Instructions before Take-off
Preparation for Take-off and Take-off Clearance

4.1 PRE-FLIGHT RADIO CHECKS

Before beginning his flight, a pilot will make certain that his radio equipment is working. The following scale of numbers will tell the pilot the quality of his radio transmissions or its readability.

Scale	Readability	Meaning
1	unreadable	terrible
2	readable now and then	good now and again
3	readable but with difficulty	fairly good
4	readable	very good
5	perfectly readable	excellent

 Listen to this

1) ACFT: Maiquetia Tower TWA 202 radio check box 1 on 119.2
   TWR: TWA 202 Maiquetia Tower readability 5

2) ACFT: Rio Tower Varig 500 radio check box 2 on 121.35
   TWR: Varig 500 Rio Tower readability 4

3) ACFT: Eldorado Tower N-20XP radio check box 1 on 121.75
   TWR: N-20XP Eldorado Tower readability 2

> **box** — radio transmitter and receiver
> **readability** — quality of transmission
> **Maiquetia** — callsign for Simon Bolivar Airport, Caracas, Venezuela
> **Rio** — Rio de Janeiro International Airport, Brazil
> **Eldorado** — Bogota International Airport, Colombia
> **TWA** — callsign for TransWorld Airlines: American airline
> **Varig** — callsign for Varig: Brazilian national airline
> **N-20XP** — callsign for a particular aircraft registered in USA

Ex. 1   Requesting a radio check

You are the pilot of a light aircraft preparing to depart from one of the following airports. In pairs, using the information below, contact the ATSU and request a radio check. Choose your callsign first.

Example   *ACFT: Santiago Tower YV-132D radio check 121.2*
             TWR: YV-132D Santiago Tower readability 5
             ACFT: YV-132D

> **callsigns**
> LV-LXD (Argentina)
> PP-VJK (Brazil)
> YV-132D (Venezuela)
> 9Y-TEA (Trinidad and Tobago)
> N105ST (USA)

> **airports**
> Aeroparque Airport (Buenos Aires, Argentina)
> Nassau International (The Bahamas)
> Quito Airport (Ecuador)
> Santiago Airport (Chile)
> La Paz Airport (Bolivia)

Ex. 2   Listening comprehension

Write down the frequencies you hear. (*Answers in Appendix 3*)

4.2 ATC CLEARANCES ——————————————————————

Before a controller gives a pilot clearance (permission) to take off, he will first give him permission to fly along a certain route, or to use certain procedures, for example, VFR (Visual Flight Rules) or IFR (Instrument Flight Rules).

ATC clearances
VFR — airspace under Visual Flight Rules
IFR — controlled airspace under Instrument Flight Rules (see map on page 19)
SID — Standard Instrument Departure

Listen to this

You will hear three ATC clearances. Listen, then you will be asked to repeat them.

1) *ATC Clearance for a Standard Instrument Departure (SID)*
   (See example on page 41.)
   ACFT: Maiquetia Mexicana 465 request clearance for Mexico City
   ATSU: Mexicana 465 cleared via flight planned route to Mexico City REKON 27 Departure, cross REKON at flight level 50 squawk 2525
   ACFT: Mexicana 465 cleared to Mexico City REKON 27 Departure, cross REKON flight level 50 squawk 2525 Mexicana 465

2) *Clearance for a VFR Flight*

   ACFT: Maiquetia Tower YV-BRL request VFR clearance to Aruba, flight time 30 minutes, endurance 3 hours
   ATSU: YV-BRL is cleared to leave the zone to the north-east VFR QNH 1002
   ACFT: Leave zone to the north-east VFR QNH 1002 YV-BRL

3) *IFR Airways Clearance*

   ACFT: Maiquetia Tower Palm 205 requests clearance to Kingston
   ATSU: Palm 205 cleared to Kingston REKON 27 Departure Red 5 Amber 10. Climb to and maintain flight level 150. Request level change en route. After departure contact Maiquetia Control on 128.5
   ACFT: Palm 205 cleared to Kingston REKON 27 Departure Red 5 Amber 10, flight level 150. Level change en route, Maiquetia Control 128.5 Palm 205

SID — an ATC departure procedure (method) which gives aircraft a route through the terminal area to the airways system after take-off. Some SIDs are named after navigational beacons, and are printed as a diagram, with departure instructions

REKON 27 Departure — name of SID

squawk — instruction to use a certain code or mode on transponder (radar equipment in aircraft) for example, squawk 2121

DME — equipment in aircraft which measures distance from a beacon on the ground

endurance — how long aircraft's fuel will last

flight time — how long flight will last

en route — part of flight between departure and approach

Mexicana — callsign for Mexicana: Mexican commercial airline

YV — Venezuelan registration

Palm — callsign for Air Florida: American commercial airline

Red 5
Amber 10 } — name of airway

flight planned route — route filed on flight plan

Ex. 1 You are the pilot of an aircraft waiting for his ATC Clearance. Listen to each clearance and then readback the clearances.

(Text of tape in Appendix 3)

4.3 START-UP AND PUSH-BACK CLEARANCE ——————

Listen to this

1) ACFT: Maiquetia Tower Viasa 505 stand B1, request start-up
   TWR: Viasa 505 start-up approved

2) ACFT: Maiquetia Tower Argentina 100 stand K15, request start-up and push-back. Information M. Our slot-time is 15 10 plus 6 minutes
   TWR: Argentina 100 start-up and push at 55

3) ACFT: Brasilia Tower Air Canada 710 on the apron, request start-up and push-back
   TWR: Air Canada 710 expect departure at 13 10 hours. Start-up at own discretion and push-back facing east

4) ACFT: La Paz Tower TWA 410 on stand D4, request push-back
   TWR: TWA 410 expect 10 minutes delay due to vehicle breakdown. Standby and monitor Ground 118.9

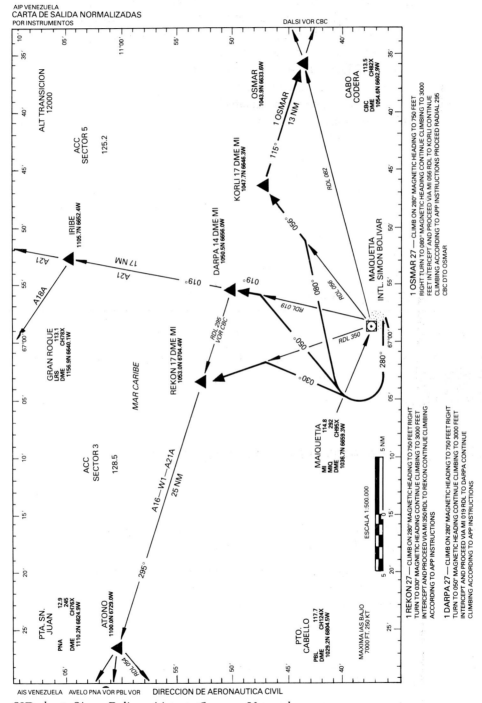

SID chart, Simon Bolivar Airport, Caracas, Venezuela
Note: This chart has been simplified and must not be used for any other purpose than the exercises in this book.

Rio Airport

start-up — to start the engines of the aircraft
at own discretion — when you want to
push-back — to push an aircraft backwards, away from the terminal
slot-time — agreed period of time for an aircraft's departure
stand — a parking space next to the terminal
breakdown — stopped working for mechanical reasons
Brasilia — Brasilia International Airport, Brazil
Argentina — callsign for Aerolineas Argentinas: Argentinian national airline
Viasa — callsign for Viasa: Venezuelan national airline
Air Canada — callsign for Air Canada: Canadian national airline

Ex. 1   **Role-play in pairs**

You are the pilot of a Boeing 747. Call the Tower and request start-up, then push-back clearance. Your partner gives clearance.

Example   *ACFT: Eldorado Tower TWA 210 on apron, request start-up*
             TWR: TWA 210 start-up approved

ACFT:	. . . Tower	TWA 210 Varig 430 Viasa 701 Clipper 900	on	stand . . . apron	request	start-up push-back

TWR:	(callsign)	push-back approved facing	south east
		start-up approved start-up engine(s) number . . . at (*time*) start-up at own discretion expect departure (*time*). Start-up at own discretion	

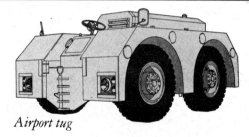

Airport tug

Ex. 2   You are the controller in the Tower at an airport. Your partner is one of the pilots of the aircraft below.

When the aircraft has contacted the Tower, answer correctly. Then change roles.

Example   *ACFT: Rio Tower N196LP on apron, request start-up*
             TWR: N196LP start-up 13 00 hours
             ACFT: N196LP start-up 13 00 hours

1) ACFT: . . . Tower N196LP on apron, request start-up
    TWR: (*time*)
    ACFT: (*readback*)

2) ACFT: . . . Tower N381DE at stand H, request start-up and push-back
    TWR: (*discretion*)
    ACFT: (*readback*)

3) ACFT: . . . Tower Varig 65 on apron, request start-up
    TWR: (*approved*)
    ACFT: (*readback*)

DC-10 on apron

4.4 TAXI INSTRUCTIONS AND HOLDING INSTRUCTIONS BEFORE TAKE-OFF

Listen to this

The surface movement controller is giving instructions to three pilots waiting to depart.

(Text in Appendix 3)

---

request taxi — pilot wishes to move his aircraft to another part of the surface movement area

holding point or **bay** — area where pilots wait for take-off clearance. The areas have numbers or letters

detailed taxi instructions — the controller gives the pilot the exact route

straight ahead — continue without turning left or right

to expedite — to do something quickly

DC-10 on taxiway

Ex. 1   **Role-play in pairs**

Imagine you are the surface movement controller (Ground) at a large airport. Give the following instructions to the pilot of the DC-10 in the photo above. Don't forget the callsign. The pilot must give the correct readback.

Example   *GROUND:*   *Viasa 101 give way to Boeing 737 entering holding bay*
               ACFT: *Viasa 101 giving way to 737*

Choose from:

> **surface movement controller**
> take first left
> turn second right
> taxi into holding bay number 7
> follow (Air France Concorde)
> give way to (TriStar) entering the apron
> give way to (Boeing 737) entering holding bay
> hold position
> hold south of runway 09
> hold short of runway
> expedite taxi

> **aircraft**
> giving way to . . .
> traffic in sight
> expediting
> following
> holding
> holding short
> first left/second right
> taxiing into holding bay 7

Ex. 2   Taxi chart

In pairs, using the taxi chart for Rio de Janeiro International Airport, one person (the pilot) requests taxi instructions to a certain point on the chart. The ground controller gives the pilot instructions. Follow these instructions along the chart and see if you arrive in the right place!

Example Your aircraft is at stand L12 on the apron. You want to go to runway 32.

ACFT: *Ground Varig 44 DC-9 stand L12, request detailed taxi instructions for runway 32*

GROUND: *Varig 44 taxi to holding point G runway 32 via taxiways L and B*

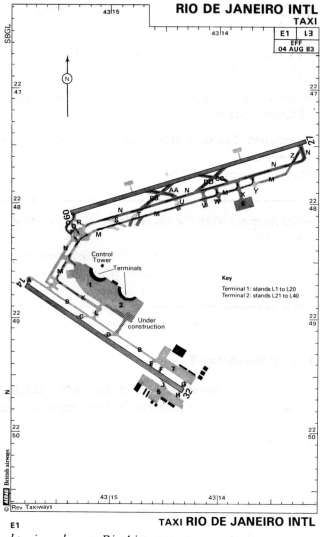

Runway and taxiway layout, Rio Airport

4.5 PREPARATION FOR TAKE-OFF AND TAKE-OFF CLEARANCE

Listen to this

1) TWR: Iberia 113 are you ready for departure?
    ACFT: Ready Iberia 113
    TWR: Iberia 113 line up and take-off immediately runway 09
    ACFT: Taking off runway 09 Iberia 113

2) TWR: LAB 808 report when ready for departure
    ACFT: Ready for departure LAB 808
    TWR: LAB 808, behind Boeing 727 on short final line up behind
    ACFT: Behind Boeing 727 on final, lining up LAB 808
    TWR: Correct LAB 808

3) TWR: Cruzeiro 51 cleared for take-off wind 240° 5 knots
    ACFT: Cleared for take-off Cruzeiro 51

4) TWR: Avianca 100 hold position. Cancel take-off due dog on runway
    ACFT: Holding Avianca 100

5) TWR: Caledonian 230 stop immediately, I say again, Caledonian 230 stop immediately
    ACFT: Stopping Caledonian 230

---

take-off — the moment when the aircraft leaves the ground (see illustration on page 18)
departure — when the aircraft is airborne (see illustration on page 18)
Cruzeiro — callsign for Cruzeiro: Brazilian domestic airline
Avianca — callsign for Avianca: Colombian airline

Ex. 1 Are you ready for departure?

The pilot of a Tupolev 154, standing short of the holding point for runway 14, is waiting for his take-off clearance. Complete the instructions and questions from the controller.

1) TWR: Lot 771 are you _____ for _____?

2) Line _____ and _____ for landing B707 to _____ runway

3) Line up _____ _____ _____ _____ 14

4) Be _____ for immediate _____

5) Cleared for _____ _____ runway 14. _____
   _____ immediately or vacate _____

6) Hold position, _____ take-off

7) Cleared _____ _____ _____ wind 230°
   7 _____

Ex. 2   **Role-play in pairs**

It is a busy morning at a small airport. Five aircraft are in the holding bay waiting to depart. In pairs, imagine you are the controller and the five pilots, and give the correct instructions and responses. Give each aircraft a callsign first, then give instructions in this order:

1 holding point, 2 enter runway, 3 take-off clearance/hold or vacate.

Example   *TWR:*   *Air India 535 report when ready for departure*
              ACFT: *Ready for departure Air India 535*
              TWR: *Air India 535 line up*
              ACFT: *Lining up Air India 535*
              TWR: *Air India 535 cleared for take-off wind 050° 4 knots. Report airborne*
              ACFT: *Air India 535 cleared for take-off. Report airborne*

CONSOLIDATION

You are a controller at Rio International Airport and your partner is a pilot. In pairs, complete the following dialogue, giving the pilot his ATC clearance, start-up and push-back clearance, taxi and take-off clearance.

ACFT: Rio Tower Varig 700 request _____ for New York on
        _____ 10 _____ M

TWR: _____ _____ cleared to _____
        _____ Esora 4 _____. _____ 4545.
        _____ time 13 25 plus _____ _____

ACFT: (*readback*) _____ _____ _____
        _____

TWR: Correct. Contact _____ on 121.9 when ready _____
        _____

ACFT: Rio Ground Varig 700 _____. start- _____ and
        push- _____

TWR: Varig 700 start- _____ and push- _____. Report
       when ready for _____

ACFT: Rio Tower Varig 700 request _____ clearance

TWR: Varig 700 taxi to holding point Z for _____ 27
       _____ taxiway M. Contact _____ on 118.0

ACFT: (*readback*) _____ _____ _____

       _____

ACFT: Rio Tower Varig 700 is taxiing on _____ M for
       _____ _____ Z

TWR: Roger Varig 700. Hold in _____

ACFT: (*readback*) _____ _____ _____

       _____

TWR: Varig 700, behind DC-10 on _____ final line up

       _____

ACFT: (*readback*) _____ _____ _____

       _____

TWR: Varig 700 cleared for take-off runway 27. _____ 240° 15
       _____. _____ airborne

ACFT: (*readback*) _____ _____ _____

       _____

Unit 5

Departing Flights

Departing Flights Transferring to Airways or Aerodrome Radar
Departing Flights Transferring from Aerodrome Radar to Airways
Departing Flights Transferring to FIS

5.1 DEPARTING FLIGHTS TRANSFERRING TO AIRWAYS OR AERODROME RADAR AFTER TAKE-OFF ————————

Listen to this

1) **TWR:** Speedbird 266 airborne 15. Climb straight ahead and contact Mexico Control 126.6
   ACFT: Climb straight ahead and contact Mexico Control 126.6 Speedbird 266

2) **TWR:** American 530 airborne 19 05. Continue on heading 050. Contact Mexico Departure 119.2
   ACFT: Heading 050 Departure 119.2 American 530

3) **TWR:** Eastern 900 airborne 28. After passing 18 000 feet, contact Mexico Control 126.6
   ACFT: Passing 18 000 feet, contact Mexico Control 126.6 Eastern 900

---

airborne 15 — the aircraft left the ground at 15 minutes past the hour, for example, 13 15

Mexico Control — Area Control Centre (ACC) directs traffic in controlled airspace

continue on — maintain same heading

Mexico Departure — a controller in Approach Radar Control directs departing flights and passes them on to the ACC

American — ⎫
Eastern — ⎬ callsigns for American commercial airlines

hand over — to instruct the aircraft to contact another ATSU

cruising level — the level maintained for most of the flight

50

Boeing 727

Shortly after the aircraft has taken off, the Tower will transfer it direct to the ACC or to the departure controller in Approach Radar Control, who, in turn, will hand over the aircraft to the ACC.

||||||||||||||||||||||||||||||||||||||||||||||||||||||||||||||||||||||||||||||||||||||||||||||||||||

Ex. 1   **Goodbye!**

Practise in pairs. The Tower has just given take-off clearance to one of the aircraft below. What time was he airborne? Give him one of the following instructions and transfer him to Airways (ACC) or to the departure controller. Aircraft gives readback.

Example   *TWR:*   *Mexicana 50 airborne 15 03. Continue on heading 090, contact Mexico Control 126.6*

   ACFT: *Heading 090, contact Mexico Control 126.6 Mexicana 50*

TWR:

Clipper 29 Lufthansa 300 TWA 250 Iberia 811 Air France 717	airborne (*time*).	Set heading 280, Turn right heading 270, Climb straight ahead, Report passing zone boundary, After passing EXRAY, On passing 2000 feet, Turn left heading 330,	contact	Mexico Control 126.6 Departure 119.2

Departure controllers at work in Approach Radar

Boeing 747 ready for take-off

5.2 DEPARTING FLIGHTS TRANSFERRING FROM AERODROME RADAR TO AIRWAYS

Listen to this

1) ACFT: Departure TWA 420 leaving flight level 180 for flight level 210
   APP: TWA 420 Contact Mexico Control 126.6
   ACFT: 126.6 TWA 420

2) ACFT: Departure American 300 passing flight level 190
   APP: American 300 identified. After passing flight level 210 turn left heading 360. Contact Mexico Control 126.6
   ACFT: Flight level 210 turn left heading 360 Mexico Control 126.6 American 300

> **identified** — the departure controller in Approach Radar Control has seen the aircraft on his radar screen (see Unit 11)
> **to intercept a radial** — see diagram on page 53
> **direct to** (a reporting point) — go straight to a point
> **Monterrey** — reporting point (near Mexico/USA border)
> **further climb** — climb to higher level
> **Aeromexico** — callsign for Aeromexico: Mexican national airline
> **Merida Control** — ACC in Mexico
> **Mazatlan Control** — ACC in Mexico

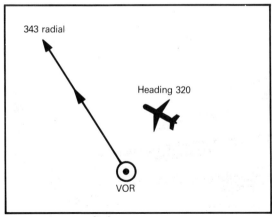

Intercepting a radial

Ex. 1   Listening comprehension

Listen to the transmission between the departure controller at Mexico Airport and a departing flight.

Now answer these questions:

1) What was the callsign of the ATSU?
2) What was the callsign of the aircraft?
3) What was the heading of the aircraft at 17 000?
4) Was the aircraft instructed to turn left or right heading 360?
5) What was the radial?

(Text of tape and answers in Appendix 3)

Boeing 747 taking off

DC-9 *in flight*

Ex. 2 **Role-play in pairs**

One person is the pilot of a departing Boeing 727, and the other is the departure controller in Approach Radar Control. Complete the following transfers:

1) ACFT: Departure Aeromexico 301 _____ flight level 150 for flight level 190

    APP: Aeromexico 301 _____ Mexico _____ on 128.5

    ACFT: (*readback*)

2) ACFT: Departure Clipper 505 _____ flight level 155

    APP: Clipper _____ _____. After _____ flight level 195 _____ right _____ 270. _____ Merida Control 125.8

    ACFT: (*readback*)

3) ACFT: Departure Mexicana 033 _____ flight level 70 for flight level 100

    APP: Mexicana 033 request _____ climb from Mexico Control _____ 128.5 at 1530

    ACFT: (*readback*)

Ex. 3 **Directions**

Say, as fast as possible, the direction of the arrow in each box. Is it pointing right or left?

5.3 DEPARTING FLIGHTS TRANSFERRING TO FIS

Listen to this

On the tape you will hear departing flights transferring to Flight Information Service and establishing communication.

1) TWR: N265AC you are now clear of controlled airspace. Contact Mexico Information on 129.9

   ACFT: Mexico N265AC 129.9

       (later)

   ACFT: Mexico Information N265AC Learjet departed Mexico City 14 00, direct to Oxaca, VMC, climbing from flight level 150 to flight level 290. Request any known conflicting traffic

   FIS: N265AC Mexico Information no reported traffic

2) TWR: PT-SBB Obregon Tower report passing zone boundary

   ACFT: Obregon Tower PT-SBB passing zone boundary

   TWR: P-BB Mazatlan QNH 1010. Contact Los Mochis Information 129.8

   ACFT: Obregon P-BB QNH 1010. 129.8 P-BB

3) ACFT: Los Mochis Information PT-ZBB Queenair departed Obregon 13 32 Z flight level 80 VFR to La Paz. Estimating La Paz 14 42 Z. Request weather La Paz

   FIS: PT-ZBB Los Mochis Information. La Paz weather not available. Call Mazatlan Control 128.0

FIS — This Flight Information Service provides useful information, such as known traffic and weather en route, for the safety of the flight (more usually VFR flights)

Mexico Information — callsign for FIS in the Mexico FIR

Learjet — type of executive jet

Uruapan and **Oxaca** — navigational beacons on Mexican airways

VMC — Visual Meteorological Conditions

IMC — Instrument Meteorological Conditions

conflicting traffic — other aircraft in the near vicinity

Z — indicating time in GMT (Greenwich Mean Time)

Los Mochis — callsign for FIS at Los Mochis, town in Mexico

XA-ACT — Mexican registration

PT-ZBB — Brazilian registration

Guadalajara — city in Mexico

met. report — weather report

Puerto Vallarta — city on Pacific coast of Mexico

Laredo and **Victoria** — cities in north-east Mexico

Doctor and **Chino** — reporting points

abeam — passing alongside

Piper Navajo

Ex. 1 **Role-play in pairs**

You are the pilot of a Piper Navajo. Contact the FIS in the Mexico FIR and request some information. The FIS acknowledges.

Choose from:

> any known conflicting traffic
> weather at Acapulco
> information of any clear air turbulence
> diversion to Guadalajara
> met. report Guadalajara

Example *ACFT:* *Mexico Information XA-DCX Navajo VFR departed Mexico City at 17 30 Z. Flight level 135 direct to Puerto Vallarta. Present position abeam Uruapan. Request met. report Guadalajara*

FIS: *XA-DCX Mexico Information roger your request. Standby*

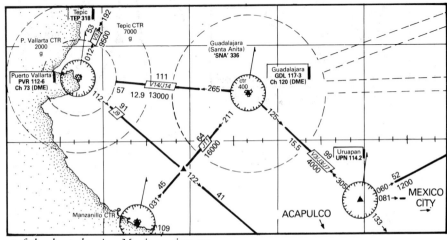

Part of the chart showing Mexican airways
Note: This chart is incomplete and must not be used for any purpose other than this exercise.

Ex. 2 In groups of *three*, using the information in the drawing and chart below, complete this transmission between the pilot of an air-taxi, the pilot of a private aircraft and the FIS at Monterrey Control.

ACFT: Monterrey Control XA-ACT Queenair from Laredo to Victoria International, abeam Doctor at this time, 15 000 feet on the Monterrey QNH 1022 VFR. ETA Chino at 23 30. Request information of any clear air turbulence activity at Chino

FIS: ....

FIS: N185KD Monterrey Information ....

.... Chino

ACFT: Monterrey Information N185KD ....

FIS: ....

FIS: XA-ACT Monterrey Information ....

....

ACFT: .... will contact you

abeam Chino XA-ACT

N185KD reports on weather to FIS

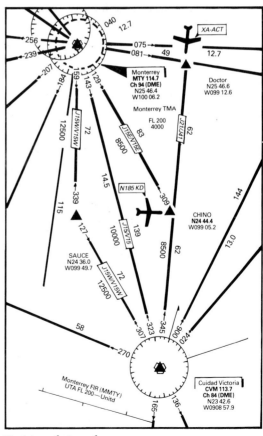

Position of aircraft

Unit 6

En Route Instructions (1)

Requesting Level Information   Level Reporting   Level Instructions
Level Change Instructions   Traffic and Weather Information and Avoidance

6.1 REQUESTING LEVEL INFORMATION

Listen to this

1) ATSU: Algerie 291 report flight level
   ACFT: Maintaining flight level 150 Algerie 291

2) ATSU: Air Malta 102 what is your altitude?
   ACFT: Passing 3000 feet Air Malta 102

3) ATSU: F-CF what is your height?
   ACFT: 1500 feet F-CF

Egyptair — callsign for Egypt Air: Egyptian national airline
Algerie — callsign for Air Algérie: Algerian national airline
Air Malta — callsign for Air Malta: Maltese national airline
ATSU — Air Traffic Service Unit, general name for all types of service, for example, FIS (see page 4)

During a flight, an ATSU may ask an aircraft for information so that the ATSU will be able to give further instructions and make certain that the aircraft maintains a safe separation from any other traffic in the vicinity. The ATSU will also ask the aircraft to report at certain levels for the same reason.

Ex. 1   How high are you?

Before giving a clearance, a controller in Approach Control wants to confirm some information. Complete the following dialogues in pairs, using the words in the box.

Example   *ATSU: F-CF report level*
               ACFT: F-CF maintaining 3000 feet

1) ATSU: Alia 300 report ....

    ACFT: ....

2) ATSU: Kuwaiti 112 what is your .... ?

    ACFT: ....

3) ATSU: Libyan 510.. ?

    ACFT: ....

4) ATSU: Cedarjet 17 .... ?

    ACFT: ....

level flight level altitude height to pass to maintain	**callsigns** Alia (Royal Jordanian Airlines) Kuwaiti (Kuwait Airways) Libyan (Libyan Arab Airlines) Cedarjet (Middle East Airlines)

6.2 LEVEL REPORTING

Listen to this

1) ATSU: Cedarjet 100 report passing flight level 90
    ACFT: Wilco Cedarjet 100 . . . Cedarjet 100 passing flight level 90

2) ATSU: Kuwaiti 323 report leaving 3000 feet, QNH is 1021
    ACFT: Report leaving 3000 feet, QNH is 1021

3) ATSU: Egyptair 909 report reaching 1500 feet, QFE is 1001
    ACFT: Wilco Egyptair 909 . . . Egyptair 909 1500 feet on QFE 1001

4) ATSU: Tunis Air 004 report passing odd levels
    ACFT: Report passing odd levels Tunis Air 004

Boeing 737

---

to reach — to arrive
odd levels — flight levels with odd numbers (eastbound), for example 70, 150, 170
even levels — flight levels with even numbers (westbound), for example 200, 280, 340
wilco — I understand your message and will follow your instructions (i.e. will comply)

Ex. 1   In pairs, one person is the controller and the other the pilot. The controller asks the pilot to report at certain levels. The pilot does so. Use the verbs in the table below:

Example *ATSU: Speedbird 303 report reaching flight level 110*
          ACFT: Wilco (later) Speedbird 303 at flight level 110

(callsign)	report	*(to leave)* *(to pass)* *(to reach)*	flight level . . .

Ex. 2   **Game**

As fast as possible, say if the following flight levels are odd or even. Read from left to right.

70	190	240	230
140	80	150	95
270	340	85	110

Jeddah Airport, Saudi Arabia

6.3 LEVEL INSTRUCTIONS

The following aircraft have just reported their levels to an Area Control Centre.

Listen to this

1) ATSU: Gulf Air 511 maintain flight level 350 to Damascus
   ACFT: Maintaining flight level 350 to Damascus Gulf Air 511

2) ATSU: Saudi 800 maintain flight level 80, expect higher in 10 miles
   ACFT: Maintaining flight level 80 Saudi 800

3) ATSU: Kuwaiti 595 maintain at least 4000 feet
   ACFT: Maintaining 4000 feet Kuwaiti 595

4) ATSU: Air Maroc 300 cross Beirut above flight level 290
   ACFT: Cross Beirut above flight level 290 Air Maroc 300

Damascus — navigational beacon and reporting point on the Syrian airways system

Beirut — navigational beacon and reporting point on the Lebanese airways system

Gulf Air — callsign for Gulf Air: airline serving some of the Gulf States

Saudi — callsign for Saudia: Saudi Arabian national airline

Air Maroc — callsign for Royal Air Maroc: Moroccan national airline

Iran Air — callsign for Iran Air: Iranian national airline

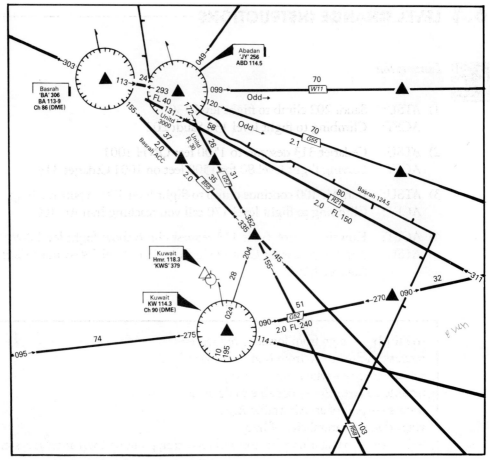

Part of the chart showing Kuwaiti airways
Note: This chart has been simplified and must not be used for any other purpose than this exercise.

Ex. 1   Imagine you are a controller at the Kuwait Area Control Centre (see chart above). The following aircraft have just reported reaching a certain level. In pairs; the pilot reports his level and is given further instructions. Don't forget the readback!

Example   *ACFT:*   *Kuwait Control TWA 606 level at flight level 100*
  ACC: *TWA 606 maintain flight level 100 and contact Basrah Control on 126.1*
  ACFT: *Flight level 100 Basrah Control 126.1 TWA 606*

ACC:	Air France 718 Speedbird 451 Clipper 50 TWA 606 Swissair 750	maintain flight level 240 until passing Basrah maintain flight level 100 and contact Basrah Control on 126.1 maintain flight level 120 until further advised cross Abadan before 1050 at flight level 170 cross Kuwait at flight level 230

6.4 LEVEL CHANGE INSTRUCTIONS

Listen to this

1) ATSU: Saudi 202 climb to flight level 130
   ACFT: Climbing to flight level 130 Saudi 202

2) ATSU: Cedarjet 313 descend to 1500 feet QNH 1001
   ACFT: Leaving flight level 80 for 1500 feet on 1001 Cedarjet 313

3) ATSU: Iran Air 100 continue climb to flight level 170, report reaching
   ACFT: Climbing to flight level 170 call you reaching Iran Air 100

4) ACFT: Kuwait Control Tunis 113 request climb above flight level 260
   ATSU: Tunis 113 Kuwait Control climb to flight level 280 contact Cairo Control 121.2

---

to climb — to go from lower to higher level
to descend — to go from higher to lower level
when ready — when you are ready
unable to comply — not able to do what you instruct
sector — part of an Air Traffic Area
Baghdad — capital city of Iraq
Samarra — navigational beacon and reporting point on Iraqi airways system

---

Ex. 1   Listen to the Area Controller giving instructions.

Now answer these questions:

1) Which flight level was Speedbird 439 leaving?

2) Which flight level was Kuwaiti 4447 leaving?

3) Which flight level was Gulf 770 asked to report passing?

4) Was Air France 818 recleared to climb or descend to flight level 130? Why did the controller repeat the instruction?

5) At which flight level was Saudi 770 asked to report?

(Text of tape and answers in Appendix 3)

Boeing 737

Ex. 2   Role-play in pairs

You are working as a sector controller in the Kuwait ACC. In pairs; the ACC instructs an aircraft to change level using the words below, and the aircraft gives a correct readback.

Example *ACC: Cedarjet 210 climb immediately to flight level 90 and report reaching*

ACFT: Climbing to flight level 90 call you reaching Cedarjet 210

ACC:	(*callsign*)	climb descend	when ready immediately at/by (*point*)	to	flight level . . . . . . feet	and report	reaching passing at (*point*)

Boeing 747

Ex. 3   In pairs, complete the following dialogue between an area controller and an en route aircraft. Look at the chart below.

ACFT: Baghdad Control Gulf 50 passing Samarra at flight level 240

ACC: ....

ACFT: Maintaining flight level 240 until Baghdad and report Gulf 50

(*later*)

ACFT: Baghdad Control Gulf 50 passing Baghdad at 36 flight level 240, estimating Hashimiyah 44

ACC: ....

ACFT: Descend to flight level 180 and report reaching Gulf 50

(*later*)

ACFT: ....

ACC: Gulf 50 maintain flight level 180 and contact Basrah Control on 125.2

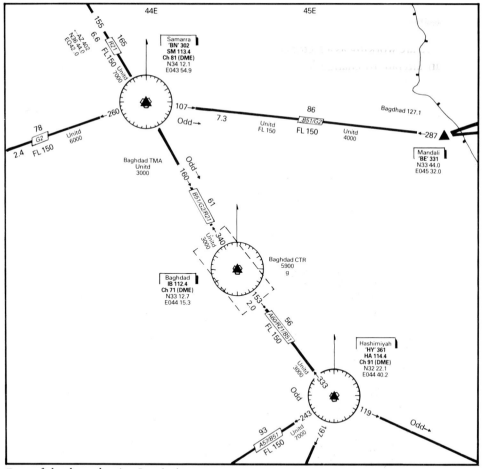

Part of the chart showing Iraqi airways
Note: This chart has been simplified and must not be used for any other purpose than this exercise.

6.5 TRAFFIC AND WEATHER INFORMATION AND AVOIDANCE —

Listen to this

1) RADAR: JY-AEX Baghdad Control, you have unknown traffic at 2 o'clock 5 miles crossing right to left

   ACFT: Looking out JY-AEX. Request vectors

   RADAR: J-EX avoiding action. Turn right 30 degrees immediately and report heading

   ACFT: Turning right 30 degrees. New heading is 090 J-EX

   RADAR: J-EX now clear of traffic. Resume own navigation to Samarra Baghdad Control

2) RADAR: Speedbird 250 Baghdad Radar we have an indication of weather 15 miles ahead of you on your present heading. A left turn of 20 degrees will take you well clear

   ACFT: Baghdad Control Speedbird 250 turning left 20 degrees on to a heading of 150

---

request vectors — pilot requests radar guidance

at 2 o'clock — position of another aircraft in relation to aircraft the controller is talking to (see diagram below)

clear of traffic — no further danger of a collision

to resume — to start again

indication of weather — CBs on radar screen

take you well clear — avoid weather

slow/fast moving — indicates speed of aircraft

closing — on collision course

overtaking — passing

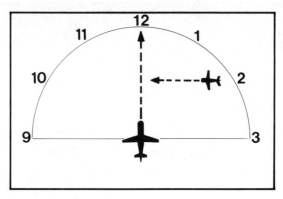

Traffic at 2 o'clock

Ex. 1   Complete the dialogues below; using the drawings, warn the pilot of Saudi 909 that there is traffic in his vicinity and instruct him how to avoid it.

  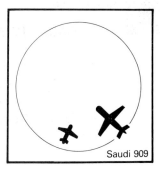

1) ATSU: Saudi 909 Baghdad Control _____ traffic at _____
   o'clock _____ miles crossing _____ to

   _____

   ACFT: Roger Saudi 909. Traffic not in sight. Request _____

2) ATSU: Saudi 909 Baghdad Control avoiding action. Turn _____
   immediately heading _____ unknown _____ at
   12 o'clock

   ACFT: Turning _____ heading _____ Saudi 909

3) ATSU: Saudi 909 Baghdad Control, unknown traffic at _____

   _____

   ACFT: Looking out Saudi 909 (*later*) Traffic in _____ Saudi 909
   ATSU: Saudi 909 Baghdad Control now clear of traffic. Resume _____
   navigation
   ACFT: Roger Saudi 909

(Answers in Appendix 3)

Boeing 747

Ex. 2   Role-play in pairs

You are a controller in the Baghdad ACC. Warn the pilots of the following aircraft about the weather conditions en route.

Example   *ATSU: Speedbird 112 Baghdad Control moderate to severe turbulence reported between flight level 70 and flight level 110*
ACFT: Roger. Request climb to flight level 130 Speedbird 112
ATSU: Speedbird 112 climb to flight level 130 report reaching
ACFT: (acknowledge)

---

aircraft
Kuwaiti 700
Cedarjet 010
Air Sudan 551
Clipper 350
Speedbird 112

---

weather information
turbulence ⎫
icing   ⎬ reported between flight level . . . and flight level . . .
radar indicates weather . . . miles ahead

Unit 7

En Route Instructions (2)

Position Reporting   Crossing and Joining Airways
Leaving Airways for Uncontrolled Airspace   En Route Holding Instructions
VOLMET Meteorological Broadcasts   Descent Clearance

7.1 POSITION REPORTING

Listen to this

1) ACFT: Santa Barbara Control Clipper 246 over Santa Barbara at 14 flight level
           330 estimating Dinty at 35
   ACC: Clipper 246 Santa Barbara roger. Climb to flight level 370 and report
           over Duets

2) ACFT: Los Angeles Control N191TX over Daggetts at 30 flight level 330
           estimating San Bernadino at 02 05
   ACC: N191TX Los Angeles Control roger. Maintain present level omit
           position reports until San Bernadino

> **Santa Barbara Control** — Area Control Centre in California, USA
> **Dinty** and **Duets** — reporting points
> **Daggetts** and **San Bernadino** — navigational beacons
> **omit position reports** — do not give position reports until instructed to do so
> **estimating** — ETO (estimated time over)
> **Goffs, Fillmore, Gorman** and **Gaviota** — navigational beacons
> **Santa Monica Control** — ACC in California
> **Santa Maria** — civil airport in California

A position report by an aircraft tells the controller the aircraft's position and time,
altitude or flight level, next position and estimated time for the next position report. So
it helps controllers to maintain traffic separation. Along the airways, pilots *must* report
at certain points, and also report at others if instructed to by a controller. (See diagram
on page 70.) If instructed by a controller, they need not report at all between certain
points.

A position report consists of: aircraft callsign, position, time over, flight level or altitude, next position and time over. The information must always be given in this order.

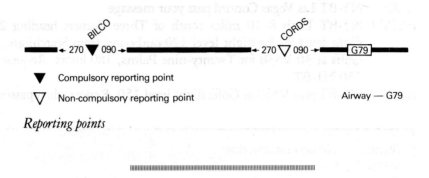

Reporting points

Ex. 1   The pilots of the aircraft below give the following position reports. They give these reports in the wrong order. Correct them!

1) ACFT: N326AB Santa Monica Control flight level 310 at 50 over Santa Monica ETO 02 15 Gorman

2) ACFT: Santa Barbara Control N421LL at 01 over Gaviota 13 000 feet estimating at 55 Santa Maria

3) ACFT: N122DE Santa Barbara Control over Fillmore flight level 190 at 25 ETA Santa Monica at 17 20

(Answers in Appendix 3)

7.2 CROSSING AND JOINING AIRWAYS

Crossing airways

Listen to this

ACFT: Los Angeles Control N121AX request airways crossing V21 at Danby
ACC: N121AX Los Angeles Control
ACFT: N121AX Cessna 310 passing Glasgow heading 010 flight level 90, VMC to cross Danby intersection at flight level 90 at 1305 N121AX
ACC: N121AX Los Angeles Control. Cross V21 at Danby before 1309 at flight level 90, maintaining own separation VMC and call when leaving the airway

Joining airways

Listen to this

ACFT: Las Vegas Control N231BT for joining clearance at Goffs

ACC: N1-BT Las Vegas Control pass your message

ACFT: N1-BT Dash 8 10 miles south of Three Corners heading 210 passing flight level 90 for flight level 120 outbound from Searchlight, estimating Goffs at 30 V538 for Twenty-nine Palms, 180 knots. Request flight level 150 N1-BT

ACC: N1-BT join V538 at Goffs flight level 150. Report when passing Goffs

---

Danby — airways intersection

V538, V21 — airways

Dash 8 — medium-sized commuter aircraft, carries 36 passengers

Three Corners, Searchlight and **Twenty-nine Palms** — airfields in California

C-GNDK — Canadian registration

All IFR flights wanting to cross or join airways (controlled airspace) have to request clearance first from either the FIS or the ACC.

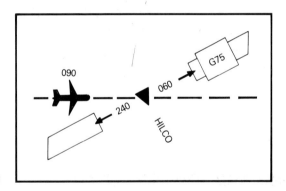

Crossing airways

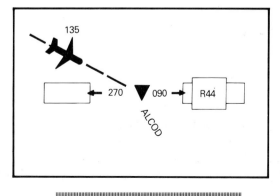

Joining airways

Ex. 1   In pairs, complete this dialogue where a pilot is asking Los Angeles Control for crossing clearance. The position of the plane is shown on the terrain chart. Fill in the missing words:

ACFT: Los Angeles Control C-GNDK _____ airways
_____ clearance _____ Lucerne

ACC: C-GNDK Los Angeles Control _____ - _____
_____

ACFT: C-GNDK Cessna 320 _____ Soggy Dry Lake
_____ 290 _____ _____ 100 VMC
_____ Lucerne at 11 15

ACC: C-GNDK Los Angeles Control, _____ V21 _____
Lucerne not before 11 15 _____ flight level 100, report when
_____ the _____

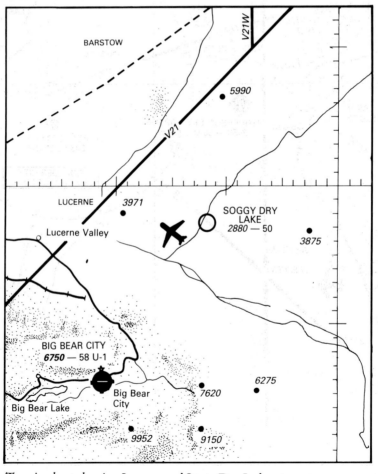

Terrain chart showing Lucerne and Soggy Dry Lake
Note: This chart must not be used for any other purpose than this exercise

Ex. 2 In pairs, complete this dialogue where a pilot is asking Las Vegas Control for joining clearance. Look at the terrain chart showing Crescent Intersection, and. fill in the missing words:

ACFT: Las Vegas Control N550SD _____ _____ clearance
_____ Crescent

ACC: 0SD Las Vegas Control _____ _____

ACFT: 0SD Cessna 310 19 _____ _____ of Crescent
_____ _____ 090 _____ _____
70 IMC _____ Jean ETO Crescent _____ 45 V
_____ for Boulder City. _____ flight level 90

ACC: 0SD _____ V _____ at _____
_____ . Flight level _____. Maintain own
_____ and contact Las Vegas Control _____ 122.1

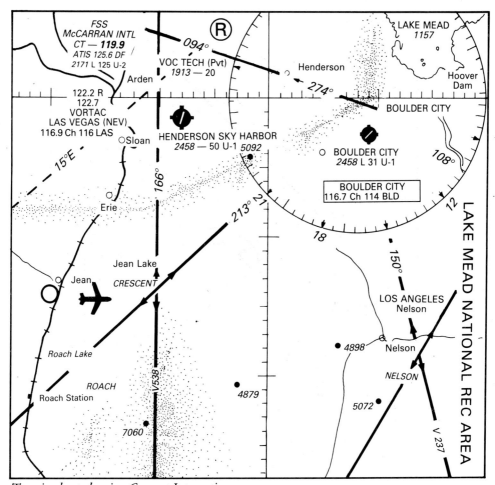

Terrain chart showing Crescent Intersection
Note: This chart must not be used for any other purpose than this exercise

7.3 LEAVING AIRWAYS FOR UNCONTROLLED AIRSPACE

Listen to this

1) ACFT: Los Angeles Control N322BX to leave control area at Channel
   ACC: N3-BX leave control area at Channel. Maintain flight level 80 to Santa Cruz. Report passing Channel

2) ACFT: Los Angeles Control N322BX to leave control area at Goleta intersection
   ACC: N3-BX leave control area at Goleta. Continue on heading 127 report passing Goleta

---

Channel, Goleta — airway intersections
Santa Cruz — small island in Santa Barbara Channel, to the south of the area shown in the chart on page 75

Los Angeles Airport

Ex. 1   Two pilots have just requested clearance to leave your control area at certain points. Give them clearance to leave, using the section of the Santa Barbara terrain chart below.

ACFT:	N-551CB XA-XCD	to leave control area at	Gaviota for Shepherd Channel for Santa Barbara Channel for Carpinteria

ACC:	*(callsign)*	leave control area at	Channel Gaviota	heading . . . to . . . Report passing (*point*)

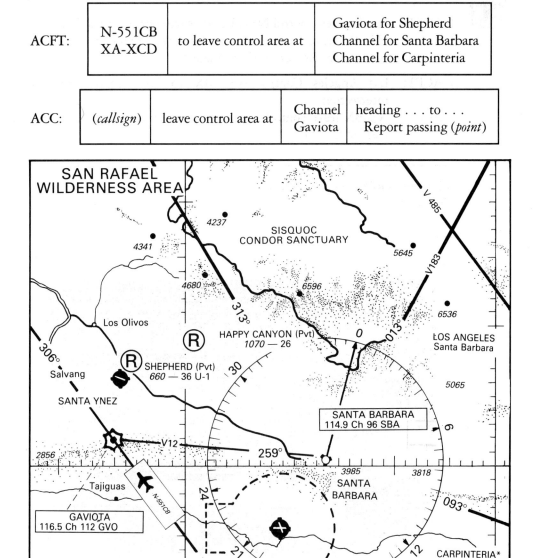

Terrain chart showing Santa Barbara
Note: This chart must not be used for any other purpose than this exercise

Ex. 2   Using the chart above, imagine you are the pilot of a Piper Saratoga on a flight over southern California. Contact the area controller and ask for clearance to cross, join and leave the control area.

7.4 EN ROUTE HOLDING INSTRUCTIONS

Listen to this

1) ACC: N243AX Santa Barbara Control
   ACFT: Santa Barbara N243AX
   ACC: 3AX maintain flight level 290 and hold at Edsel. Expect further clearance at 20
   ACFT: 3AX maintaining flight level 290 and holding at Edsel

2) ACFT: Santa Barbara Control 3AX holding at Edsel flight level 290
   ACC: 3AX roger, your expected approach time 25 due traffic

3) ACC: United 401Q Santa Barbara Control
   ACFT: Santa Barbara Control United 401Q
   ACC: United 401Q due traffic congestion make one right-hand orbit in your present position and leave on heading 180
   ACFT: Right-hand orbit and leave on heading 180 United 401Q

---

to hold — to stay over a particular point while waiting for further clearance from air traffic control (see diagram on page 98)
Hilco, Foots and **Edsel** — reporting points on airways over Pacific Ocean
hold at — to begin the holding procedure
401Q — 'Q' after a callsign means the aircraft's flight plan has been revised
right-hand orbit — to fly in a circle, turning to the right
right-hand pattern inbound track — description of a hold (see diagram on page 77)
VOR — Very high frequency Omnidirectional Range beacon, for example, Santa Barbara

VOR with DME

For a variety of reasons, such as bad weather (for example, fog), or heavy traffic in the Terminal Manoeuvring Area or on the airways, an emergency descent, or traffic crossing, aircraft are sometimes asked to delay their approach or en route flight by 'holding' over a certain point until the controllers give them clearance to proceed.

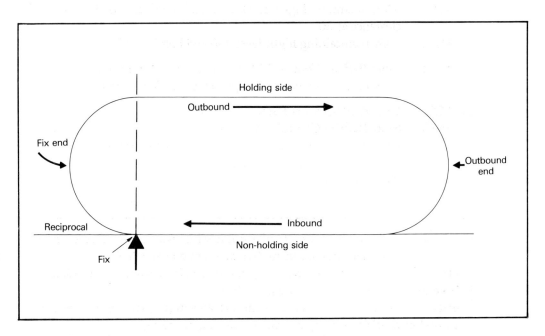

A typical holding pattern

Ex. 1   Listen to the controller giving two pilots holding instructions.

Then answer these questions:

1) Was American 326 instructed to descend or climb?
2) Was the aircraft to be at flight level 310 by Foots or flight level 210?
3) Was the heading of the inbound track 322 or 332?
4) Was the inbound track 069 or 249?
5) Was the aircraft told to hold between 15 and 35 DME or 15 and 25 DME?

(Text of tape and answers in Appendix 3)

DC-10

Ex. 2   Wait a minute!

You are a controller at Los Angeles Control Centre giving holding instructions to the following aircraft. Use the information below to complete the instructions.

callsigns	reporting points	flight levels
American	Duets	290
Caledonian	Edsel	310
Delta	Foots	330
Clipper		
United		

1) ACC: (*callsign*)   maintain _____ _____ _____
and   hold   at _____ . Expect   further _____ at
_____ . No further _____ expected

2) ACC: (*callsign*) descend to _____ _____ _____
to be over _____ at flight level _____ inbound
_____ 240. _____ -hand pattern outbound time
_____ minutes

3) ACC: (*callsign*)   hold   on   the   150   radial   of   the   Santa   Barbara
_____ at   30   miles _____ . Inbound   track   199
right-hand _____

Ex. 3   Role-play in pairs

Now, in pairs, give these instructions again and the readback.

7.5 VOLMET METEOROLOGICAL BROADCASTS

During a flight, the pilot may wish to know the weather conditions at the aerodrome of his destination. He can listen to VOLMET broadcasts which are continuous and contain information about certain airports in a particular region.

The meanings of abbreviations you may hear in VOLMET broadcasts are given below:

CAVOK — ceiling and visibility OK (say it KAV-O-KAY)
FRONT — a front, for example, a warm or cold front
GRADU — gradual, slowly
INTER — intermittent, not continuous
NIL — none
NOSIG — no significant change, not much change
OBS — observe or observation
PROB — probability
RAPID — rapid, very fast
SIGMET — significant information about weather, for example, a hurricane
SNOCLO — aerodrome closed due to snow
SNOWTAM — notam (Notice for Airmen) about snow clearing at aerodrome
SPECIAL — special meteorological report
SPOT — spot wind
TEMPO — temporarily, for a short period
TREND — trend or tending to go in a certain direction
TIL — until

Listen to this example of part of a VOLMET broadcast.

(Text in Appendix 3)

---

octa — the sky is divided into eight parts (see diagram on page 80) to show the density of the cloud cover
Geneva, Zurich and **Basle** — airports in Switzerland
BREAK — new message beginning (to another aircraft)
in haze — misty
fog patches — areas of fog

Amount of sky covered	0	1/8	2/8	3/8	4/8	5/8	6/8	7/8	8/8	Sky obscured
Symbol	○	◑	◖	◗	◐	◒	◓	◑	●	⊗

Octas

Ex. 1   Listening comprehension

Listen to the example of part of a VOLMET broadcast from Nicosia, in Cyprus. Then answer these questions:

1) What time was the Larnaca met. report issued?
2) Was there any wind at Athens?
3) What was the surface wind speed at Rhodes?
4) What was the direction and speed of the wind at Ben Gurion?
5) What was the QNH for Ramat David?

(Text of tape and answers in Appendix 3)

Ex. 2   Listen to the second part of the VOLMET broadcast.

Now can you answer these questions?

1) Was the visibility at Beirut
   a) 1 km?
   b) 110 km?
   c) 10 km?
   d) 5 km?

2) Was the temperature at Damascus
   a) −3?
   b) −03?
   c) −04?
   d) 03?

3) At Cairo, at 2100 metres were there

    a) 3 octas?
    b) 2 octas?
    c) 4 octas?
    d) 8 octas?

4) Was the QNH at Istanbul

    a) 1012?
    b) 1112?
    c) 1002?
    d) 1021?

(Text of tape and answers in Appendix 3)

Ex.3   **Practice**

Imagine you are asked to record part of a VOLMET broadcast transmitted by Auckland VOLMET, New Zealand. Read it aloud, slowly and clearly:

All Stations, All Stations Auckland VOLMET

Met. Report:	Auckland 2200, wind 240° 12 knots, visibility 50 kilometres, 4 octas 1800 feet, 6 octas 3000 feet. Temperature 19, dewpoint 12, QNH 1017 nosig
Met. Report:	Christchurch 2200, wind 200° 07 knots, visibility 6 kilometres, haze. 2 octas 2500 feet. Temperature 13, dewpoint 07, QNH 1011 nosig
Met. Report:	Wellington 2200, wind 190° 08 knots, visibility 60 kilometres. 1 octa 3000 feet. Temperature 17, dewpoint 12, QNH 1011 nosig
Met. Report:	Tahiti 2130, wind 280° 05 knots, visibility 10 kilometres or better. 3 octas 2000 feet. Temperature 30, dewpoint 24, QNH 1012 nosig

Boeing 737

7.6 DESCENT CLEARANCE

Listen to this

1) ACFT: Los Angeles Control Speedbird 505 passing Edsel at flight level 210. Request descent at 1705

   ACC: Speedbird 505 Los Angeles Control descend immediately to flight level 120. Report passing flight level 150

   ACFT: Speedbird 505 leaving flight level 210 for flight level 120. Report passing flight level 150

2) ACFT: Los Angeles Control TWA 310 over Edtoo 15 flight level 270, request descent

   ACC: TWA 310 maintain flight level 270. Expect descent at 20

   ACFT: TWA 310 maintaining flight level 270 and standing-by for descent

3) ACC: TWA 310 Los Angeles Control descend to flight level 120. Expedite descent through flight level 270 to flight level 190 to be level 10 miles south of Perch. Report passing 190

   ACFT: TWA 310 descend to flight level 120, expediting descent through flight level 270 to flight level 190 to be level 10 miles south of Perch. Report passing flight level 190

Perch — reporting point on 249 radial of LAX VOR
Edtoo — non-compulsory reporting point on R77

Boeing 767

Ex.1   Going down!

You are a controller at Los Angeles ACC. Give the following instructions to pilots requesting descent clearance:

ACC:	(callsign)	Maintain level. Standby for descent at 50
		Expect descent clearance in 10 minutes
		Change to 121.0 and request descent
		Start descent to flight level 120 in 5 miles, report passing flight level 190
		Expect descent clearance in 15 miles
		Start descent to flight level 180 immediately
		Expedite descent through flight level 190 to flight level 150
		Descend to flight level 100 to be level 20 miles south of Foots

Ex. 2   United 401 is en route from Honolulu to Los Angeles. Imagine you are the pilot and request clearance to begin your descent. The ACC uses the clearances in Ex. 1.

Example   *ACFT: Los Angeles Control United 401 Foots flight level 310 request descent*
             ACC: United 401 Los Angeles descend to flight level 150. Report passing flight level 190
             ACFT: (readback)

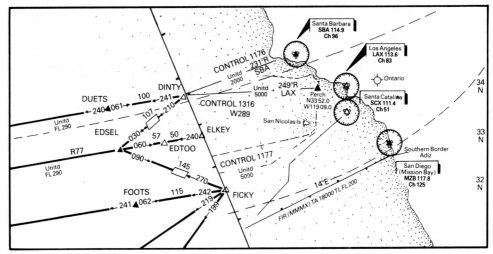

Part of the chart showing Pacific airways
Note: This chart is incomplete and must not be used for any other purpose than the exercises in this book.

Unit 8

Approach/Zone Control – VFR Flights

Initial Contact   Circuit Joining Instructions
Reporting in the Aerodrome Traffic Circuit   Landing Instructions

8.1 INITIAL CONTACT

Listen to this

1) ACFT: Mombasa Approach 5Y-CCD
   APP: 5-CD Mombasa Approach go ahead
   ACFT: Mombasa 5-CD Beechcraft Baron 20 miles north-east of your field.
           Heading 250 at 8000 feet descending. VFR from Malindi to
           Mombasa, estimating Mombasa at 35, request joining instructions

2) ACFT: Malindi Tower 5Y-CCE
   APP: 5-CE Malindi Tower go ahead
   ACFT: Malindi 5-CE Cessna 310, 30 miles north of Mombasa at 6000 feet.
           VFR from Pemba to Malindi, estimating overhead Malindi 1402 for
           landing

5Y-CCD — Kenyan registration
Mombasa and **Malindi** — airfields on Kenyan coast (see chart on page 85)
Pemba — airfield on the island of Pemba, off Tanzania
joining instructions — instructions to enter controlled airspace
Beechcraft Baron and **Cessna 310** — light aircraft
for landing — request for instructions to enter aerodrome traffic circuit
Tanga — airfield on the coast of Tanzania

On approach to the aerodrome, the pilot first contacts the controller in order to give him details of the aircraft and route and to warn the controller of his intention to enter the traffic circuit, and land.

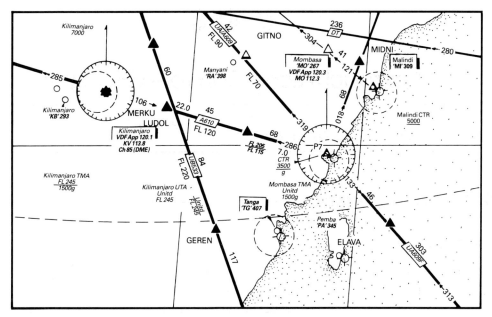

Part of the chart showing East African airways
Note: This chart is incomplete and must not be used for any other purpose than this exercise.

Ex. 1   Listening comprehension

Listen to these two pilots making their initial contact with the Tower and passing their details and route. Look at the East African chart. Then answer these questions.

1) Was 5Y-CDD
   a) 25 miles
   b) 35 miles   } east of Tanga airfield?
   c) 45 miles
   d) 55 miles

2) Was the heading
   a) 180?
   b) 080?
   c) 280?
   d) 290?

3) Was the level
   a) 4000 feet?
   b) 6000 feet?
   c) 7000 feet?
   d) 5000 feet?

4) Was the ETA for Tanga
    a) 10 19?
    b) 10 09?
    c) 10 00?
    d) 10 11?

5) Was the position of 5Y-CCD 20 miles south-west or south-east of Mombasa?

6) Was it flying from Malindi to Pemba or Mombasa to Pemba?

7) Was the QNH 1022 or 1021?

8) Was the ETA over Pemba 23 or 32?

(Text of tape and answers in Appendix 3)

Ex. 2   Role-play in pairs

Using the chart on page 85, contact Approach or the Tower and pass your details and route. Choose two of the following routes:

> Tanga to Mombasa
> Pemba to Mombasa
> Mombasa to Malindi
> Malindi to Pemba
> Malindi to Tanga
> (or the other way around!)

Mombasa Airport, Kenya

8.2 CIRCUIT JOINING INSTRUCTIONS

Listen to this

1) ACFT: Malindi Tower 5Y-AAB 10 miles north of your field. 3000 feet for landing

   TWR: 5Y-AAB Malindi join downwind number 1, runway 03 wind 030° 10 knots temperature 25 QNH 1012. Report downwind

2) ACFT: Malindi Tower 5Y-CCL overhead at 4000 feet for landing

   TWR: 5Y-CCL descend to circuit height 1000 feet QFE 1006. Join left-hand downwind, runway 21 wind calm. Number 2 in traffic. Report downwind

---

to join — enter aerodrome traffic circuit

number 2 in traffic — the aircraft is the second to land

circuit height — height at which aircraft join circuit

report downwind — position on circuit where pilot should report (see diagram on page 90)

right-hand/left-hand — direction of circuit

turning base — aircraft turning onto base leg of circuit (see diagram on page 90)

Usually there are a number of aircraft in the circuit, and so the controller has to give each one a sequence number in the traffic circuit for landing, in order to avoid collisions. He will at the same time pass information on the preceding traffic.

Ex. 1   Role-play in pairs

You are the controller in the Tower at Mombasa. Pass the following joining instructions to the aircraft which have just contacted you:

Example *TWR:*   *5Y-CCB join right-hand downwind number 2, runway 21 wind calm, temperature 24 QNH 1019. Report downwind*

   ACFT: *5Y-CCB runway 21 QNH 1019. Reporting downwind*

TWR:	(*callsign*) join	left-hand right-hand	downwind	number . . . runway . . .
		crosswind base		

Surface wind	calm 040° 5 knots 220° 10 knots 020° 8 knots	temperature	24 27 25	QFE QNH	1020 1019 1022	Report . . .

ACFT: (*Readback and callsign*)

Ex. 2   Practice

You are a controller in the Tower at Malindi. Complete the following joining instructions, using words from the list below.

1) TWR: _____-CD _____ to circuit _____ 2000
    feet. Join _____ number 2 _____ 03.
    _____ wind 045° 4 _____ . _____ 27
    QFE 1015 _____ . Report _____ .
    Cessna turning base
    ACFT: (*callsign*) _____ _____

2) TWR: _____-CD join _____ _____ downwind
    number 1 runway 21 wind _____ . _____ 25
    QNH 1005 _____ . _____ downwind
    ACFT: Number 1 _____ 21. Reporting _____ (*callsign*)

climb	altitude	downwind	runway	miles	speed	calm
descend	height	upwind	surface	knots	temperature	
base	report	right-hand	for	hectopascals	turning	

8.3 REPORTING IN THE AERODROME TRAFFIC CIRCUIT —————

Listen to this

1) ACFT: Malindi Approach 5Y-CCD joining downwind. Aerodrome in sight, request visual approach runway 35

   APP: 5Y-CCD cleared visual approach runway 35, number 3 to land, contact Tower on 119.6

2) ACFT: Malindi Approach 5-CD turning final

   APP: 5-CD continue approach, report on long final, number 2 to a Cessna crossing the threshold. Contact Tower on 118.5

   ACFT: Malindi roger 118.5

3) ACFT: Malindi Tower 5Y-CCD long final

   TWR: 5-CD roger. Report final

---

aerodrome in sight — airfield is visible from aircraft
visual approach — an approach to land without assistance from ATC, i.e. radar
               vectors
turning final — aircraft turning onto its final approach (see diagram on page 90)
long final — the report is made when aircraft turns onto final approach at a
             distance greater than 4 nautical miles from touchdown. (Short
             final is a position from about 2 nautical miles to touchdown,
             although not defined)
circle the aerodrome — fly in 360° circles over aerodrome
orbit — circle
leg — section of circuit, for example, base leg

Reports are made at certain positions in the circuit so that the controller knows the positions of all the aircraft. He can, therefore, advise a pilot of the traffic situation, so the pilot can maintain safe separation.

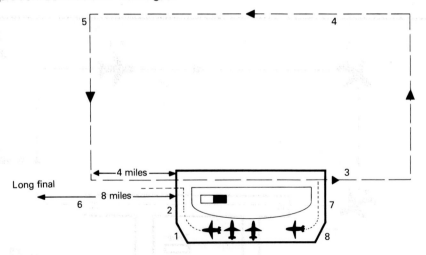

1 Preflight checks and taxi clearance   5 Base leg report (only if requested)
2 Request take-off clearance   6 Final report
3 Airborne report   7 Runway vacated report
4 Downwind report   8 Parking instructions

Reporting points on aerodrome traffic circuit

Ex.1   You are a controller in Tanga Tower. Issue the following clearances to the aircraft which have just reported their positions in the circuit: 5-CE   5-BB   5-CC   5-CD

Example *ACFT: Tanga Tower 5-CC downwind*
             TWR: 5-CC continue approach, report turning final

TWR:	5-CE 5-BB 5-CC 5-CD	continue approach, report long final, number 3 to land report turning final make a right-hand orbit and report downwind report turning base report turning long final circle the aerodrome and report downwind traffic 3 miles ahead on downwind leg traffic on straight-in-approach on 6-mile final cleared to final runway 35 number 2 to land, number 1 on final

Ex.2   Work in pairs, using the drawing on page 91, showing three aircraft in the traffic circuit and one aircraft joining the circuit. The pilots report their positions and wait for further instructions.

Example *ACFT: Tower 5-CF turning final*
             TWR: 5-CF continue approach, report 6-mile final. Number 1 to land
             ACFT: (readback)

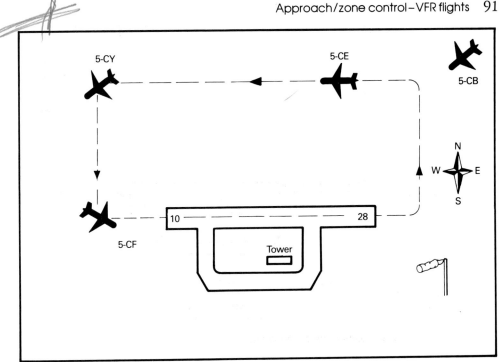

Traffic circuit for Exercise 2

8.4 LANDING INSTRUCTIONS ────────────────────────

Listen to this

1) ACFT: Malindi Tower 5-CD aerodrome in sight, request straight-in-approach on runway 35
   TWR: 5-CD cleared straight-in-approach runway 35. Wind calm. Temperature 27 QFE 1002. Report final

2) ACFT: Malindi 5-CD short final
   TWR: 5-CD cleared to land, surface wind 240° 10 knots

3) ACFT: Malindi Tower 5-CB long final
   TWR: 5-CB continue approach, traffic departing and one ahead to land. Report on 4-mile final

4) ACFT: Malindi 5-CB 4-mile final
   TWR: 5-CB cleared to land, wind 330° 12 knots

Ex. 1   The following aircraft have just reported that they are on approach to Pemba. Complete the dialogues below by passing them their landing clearance, weather and traffic information, using the information and drawings below. Add the readback.

1) ACFT: Pemba 5-CX aerodrome in sight, request straight-in-approach
    TWR: 5-CX . . . .
    ACFT: (*readback*)

2) ACFT: Pemba 5-CT long final
    TWR: . . . .
    ACFT: (*readback*)

3) ACFT: Pemba 5-CO on 10 mile final
    TWR: . . . .
    ACFT: (*readback*)

4) ACFT: Pemba 5-CM turning final
    TWR: . . . .
    ACFT: (*readback*)

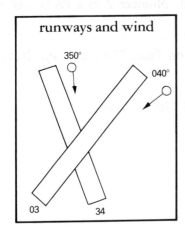

runways and wind

350°

040°

03   34

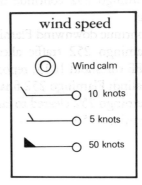

wind speed

Wind calm

10 knots

5 knots

50 knots

27°C

24°C

traffic information	QFE/QNH
departing	1018
one ahead to land	1007
one turning base	1020

make a straight-in-approach
cleared to land
continue approach . . . report
make a 360° turn to the right, report downwind

CONSOLIDATION

Read the dialogue in groups of three (ACFT, APP and TWR).

ACFT: Malindi Approach Flamingo 252
APP: Flamingo 252
ACFT: Malindi Flamingo 252 is an F-27 15 miles south of your field heading 020, from Pemba to Malindi, 5000 feet on QNH 1017 ETA Malindi 25 for landing
APP: Flamingo 252 cleared to Malindi VFR to join left-hand downwind runway 17, wind 170° 15 knots. QFE 1015. Call joining downwind

(later)

ACFT: Malindi Flamingo 252 downwind
APP: Flamingo 252 contact Tower on 119.6 for landing instructions
ACFT: Flamingo 252 contacting Tower 119.6
ACFT: Malindi Tower Flamingo 252 downwind runway 17
TWR: Flamingo 252 continue downwind. Number 2 to a PA23 turning base leg
ACFT: Continue downwind Flamingo 252
TWR: Flamingo 252 traffic ahead now on final. Turn base leg. Runway 17 QFE threshold 1015, report final
ACFT: Malindi Flamingo 252 final
TWR: Flamingo 252 cleared to land, wind 170° 15 knots
ACFT: Flamingo 252

Unit 9

Approach/Zone Control – IFR Flights

ATIS for Arriving/Departing Flights   Initial Approach Clearance

9.1 ATIS FOR ARRIVING/DEPARTING FLIGHTS

In Unit 3.1 you heard examples of ATIS (Automatic Terminal Information Service) broadcasts for departing flights only. The majority of large airports have one service: for arriving and departing flights. The information which the pilot needs is generally the same for inbound and outbound flights and they also have the same alphabetical system of coding.

Athens, Dusseldorf, Istanbul, Madrid, Riyadh, Vienna, Harare, Jeddah, Lagos, Lusaka, Brasilia, Houston, are just a few examples of international airports with an ATIS facility.

ILGS approach — Instrument Landing Guidance System. IGS approach, a special kind of ILS (see unit 10.1), is used in Hong Kong

wind **variable** — direction of wind changes

transition level — (for inbound flights) For example, flight level 70: at flight level 70 change altimeter setting from 1013.2 to QNH

transition altitude — (for outbound flights) For example, 7000 feet: on passing 7000 feet QNH change to 1013.2

 Listen to this example of an ATIS broadcast from Kai Tak Airport, Hong Kong.

Ex. 1   Fill in the missing words from the ATIS broadcast you have just heard:

Hong Kong _____ Airport information _____. Runway-in-_____ 13.   Expect   IGS _____. _____ wind 090 _____ 120° at _____ knots, visibility _____ kilometres,   present   weather _____.   Cloud 1 _____ at _____ feet.   Temperature _____, QNH _____ millibars. Acknowledge _____ _____ on   frequencies _____ for _____ and _____ for _____

(Text of tape in Appendix 3)

Kai Tak Airport, Hong Kong

Ex. 2   Listen to another ATIS broadcast and then answer the questions below:

1) Which airport is transmitting the ATIS broadcast?
2) What is the code letter?
3) Is runway 29 for landing or departing aircraft?
4) What is the transition level?
5) What is the wind speed?
6) What is the visibility?
7) How many octas of cloud are at 800 metres?
8) At what height are there 5 octas of cloud?
9) What is the dewpoint?
10) In millibars, what are the QNH and QFE?

(Text of tape and answers in Appendix 3)

9.2 INITIAL APPROACH CLEARANCE

 Listen to this

ACFT: Narita Arrival Japanair 431 heavy with B
RADAR: Japanair 431 Narita maintain flight level 100 cleared to Onjuku, Standard Jupiter One arrival. After passing Onjuku, descend to 8000 feet QNH 992. Number 3 in traffic. No delay expected, present information is C. Visibility 6 kilometres in haze
ACFT: Narita Japanair 431 Standard Jupiter One arrival. After passing Onjuku cleared to leave flight level 100 for 8000 feet QNH 992. Japanair 431
RADAR: Japanair 431 correct. Squawk 5616 ident

Narita Arrival — Approach Radar Control at Narita Airport, Tokyo
heavy — a large plane, for example, DC-10 or Boeing 747 (B is the ATIS code for arriving aircraft)
Onjuku — VOR
Jupiter One arrival — name of STAR (Standard Terminal Arrival Route)
squawk . . . ident — to use identification signal as well as code, i.e. 5616 plus 'blip' appears on radar screen (see Unit 11)
Jupiter and **Martin** — reporting points
drizzle — light rain with mist

Narita Airport, Tokyo

You have just heard an example of an approach radar controller clearing an aircraft to commence its initial approach to Narita Airport for an instrument approach. The controller will not give the pilot a full clearance as he will have the approach procedure instructions in the STAR. These procedures will guide the aircraft directly to a holding point. Occasionally, however, the controller may change the procedures and clear the aircraft by a different route.

Controllers in the Tower at Narita

Ex. 1   Listening comprehension

You are the pilot of an aircraft on approach to Narita Airport. Listen to the following instructions and give the readback.

(*Text of tape in Appendix 3*)

> **BREAK, BREAK** — controller is starting a new message and addressing a new addressee

Ex. 2   Look at the diagram of a holding stack below. In the last exercise, Speedbird 301 was cleared to enter the hold at Lake. It is number 6 in traffic and is level at 8000 feet. Complete the dialogue below in groups of four (there are two arrival controllers):

ACFT (1):   Speedbird 301 entering the hold. Maintaining 8000 feet

ARRIVAL (1):   Speedbird _____ _____ in   the   hold
                _____ 6000 _____. Expect _____
                _____ at _____.   Report _____
                7000 feet

ACFT (1):   Speedbird 301 leaving 8000 feet for 6000 feet
                (*later*) Speedbird 301 passing _____ feet
                (*later*) Speedbird 301 at _____ feet

ARRIVAL (1):   _____ 301 _____ _____ 3000
                _____. Contact _____ on 118.9

ACFT (2):   Narita Approach Japanair 510 at 5000 feet!

ARRIVAL (2):   Speedbird 301 _____ _____ immediately, I
                _____ _____, stop _____.
                _____ _____ feet.   BREAK,   BREAK
                Japanair 510 descend now to 3000 feet QNH 1030 and
                leave Jupiter heading 360

ACFT (2):   ....

AIRWAYS

Flight level 80

7000 feet

6000 feet

5000 feet

4000 feet

3000 feet

2000 feet

Holding stack

Game — Bravo Charlie November!

Look at the diagram below showing some of the airways over Italy. Name the beacons using the phonetic callsigns only. (There are nine VORs, DMEs and NDBs.)

Example *Voghera — VICTOR OSCAR GOLF*

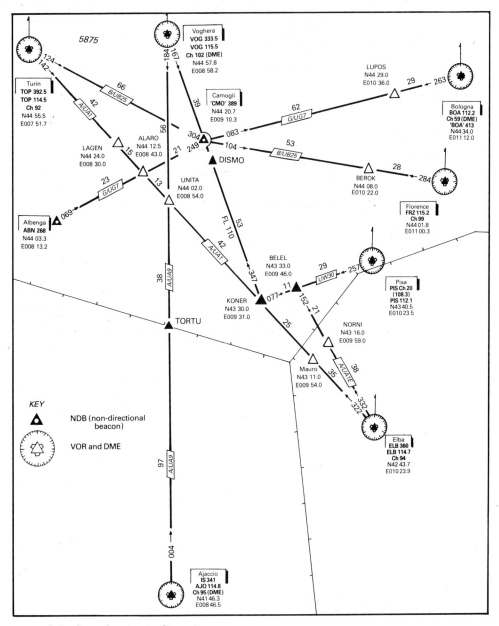

Part of the chart showing Italian airways
Note: This chart is incomplete and must not be used for any other purpose than this exercise.

Unit 10

Approach and Landing Instructions – IFR Flights

Intermediate and Final Approach   Landing Clearance
Taxi Instructions after Landing   Missed Approach   Diversions

10.1 INTERMEDIATE AND FINAL APPROACH

Listen to this

ACFT: Narita Approach Japanair 402 approaching Choshi 6000 feet
APP: Japanair 402 leave Choshi heading 319 for Lake, contact Arrival
            125.8. Report heading
ACFT: Heading 319 changing to 125.8 Japanair 402

...

ACFT: Narita Approach Japanair 402 heading 319 6000 feet
ARRIVAL: Japanair 402 Narita Arrival maintain 6000 feet. Radar vectoring
            ILS Approach runway 16 QNH 1030
ACFT: 6000 feet runway 16 QNH 1030 Japanair 402

(later)

ARRIVAL: Japanair 402 descend to 3000 feet, range 20 miles from
            touchdown. Fly heading 330, report passing 4000 feet
ACFT: Leaving 6000 feet for 3000 feet heading 330. Report passing
            4000 feet Japanair 402

(later)

ARRIVAL: Japanair 402 turn left heading 210 to intercept ILS runway 16.
            Report established on localiser
ACFT: Turning left heading 210, report established runway 16 Japanair
            402

(later)

ACFT: Narita Arrival Japanair 402 established on the localiser
ARRIVAL: Japanair 402 descend on the glide path. Maintain not less than
            170 knots to outer marker, contact Tower 121.8
ACFT: Not less than 170 knots to outer marker, contact Tower 121.8
            Japanair 402

ILS — Instrument Landing System — electronic equipment which guides a pilot onto the runway, using two sets of radio beams transmitted from the ground near the runway (see diagram below)

to be established on {
   the localiser — to be in line with the extended centreline of the runway (see diagram below)
   the glide path — to be on the glide path (see diagram below)
}

glide slope — glide path

outer marker — a radio beacon marking the given distance to the threshold. A beam intercepts the localiser beam vertically at a given height, helping the pilot to check he is on the correct glide path (see diagram below)

closing — to come towards the centreline of the runway

range — distance

reduce your speed — go slower

Choshi — VOR

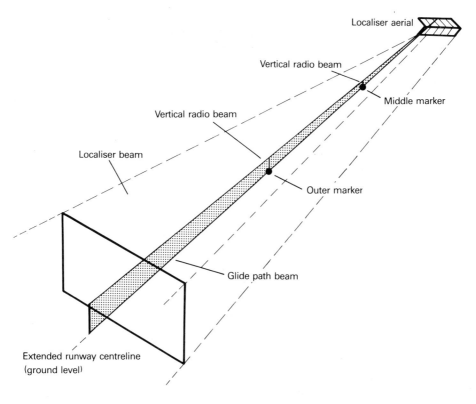

Instrument Landing System

Ex. 1   In groups of four, imagine you are the two controllers in Approach Radar Control who guide the aircraft during the intermediate and final approach stages of a flight, and the pilots of two aircraft on approach to a large international airport. Complete the following dialogue. Here are some words to help you:

range heading	marker ILS	speed outer

descent/descend established	touchdown reduce

ACFT (1):   Narita Approach Japanair 426 at flight level 80

APP: Japanair 426 _____ to 6000 feet QNH 1006. 18 miles from _____

ACFT (1):   _____ flight level 80, _____ to 6000 feet _____ 1006 Japanair 426

APP: Japanair 426 report speed

ACFT (1):   230 knots and reducing to 190 knots Japanair 426

APP: Japanair 426 roger. _____ your _____ to 170 knots

ACFT (1):   170 knots Japanair 426

APP: Japanair 426 _____ left heading 272

ACFT (1):   Left heading 272 Japanair 426

ACFT (2):   Narita Approach Air France 600 at flight level 100

APP: Japanair 426 contact Arrival on 120.4. BREAK, BREAK. Air France 600 _____ to flight level 80 and _____ on reaching

ACFT (1):   120.4 Japanair 426

ACFT (2):   _____ flight level 100 for flight level 80 Air France 600

ACFT (1):   Arrival Japanair 426 _____ 272

ARR: Japanair   426   continue _____ _____. _____ 13 miles, runway 16

ACFT (1):   Heading _____ Japanair 426

ARR: Japanair 426 descend to 2800 feet

ACFT (1):   Descending to 2800 feet Japanair 426

ARR: Japanair 426 reduce speed to 160 knots and maintain to the _____

ACFT (1):   Reducing to 160 knots and maintaining to the _____ _____ Japanair 426

ARR: Japanair 426 turn left heading 210. Report _____ _____ _____ _____ runway 16

ACFT (1): _____ 210 _____ _____ on the
_____ Japanair 426

ACFT (2): Narita Arrival Air France 600 flight level 80 heading 210

ARR: Air France 600 continue present _____ 14 miles from
touchdown, runway 16

ACFT (2): Continue heading 210 Air France 600

ACFT (1): Japanair 426 _____ on the ILS

ARR: Roger, your _____ is 10 miles from touchdown, continue
_____ on the _____ _____ 160 knots
to the outer marker. Contact Tower on 118.7

ACFT (1): 118.7 Japanair 426

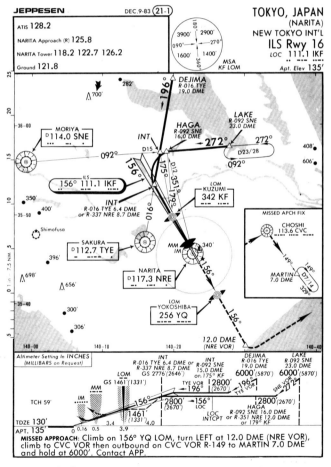

Approach chart — ILS

Localiser

10.2 LANDING CLEARANCE

Listen to this

ACFT: Narita Tower Cathay 50 is fully established, runway 16
TWR: Cathay 50 report passing outer marker. QFE 1010 wind 180° 15 knots
ACFT: Report passing outer marker QFE 1010, Cathay 50

(*later*)

ACFT: Outer marker Cathay 50
TWR: Cathay 50 continue approach, one DC-10 to depart
ACFT: Continue approach Cathay 50
TWR: Cathay 50 cleared to land
ACFT: Cleared to land Cathay 50
TWR: Cathay 50 Landing-time 23. Take first right and contact Ground on 121.8 when vacated

---

is fully established — the aircraft is in line with the localiser beam and on the glide path
landing-time — exact time of touchdown
vacated — aircraft has left the runway in use

Ex. 1   Role-play in pairs

One person is the Controller in the Tower and the other is the pilot of one of the landing aircraft. Complete the dialogue using the information below, choosing your own landing-time!

aircraft	wind	speed	QFE	run-
Speedbird 505			1002	way
Japanair 402	270 ← 090		998	16
Cathay 50			1021	34

ACFT: Narita _____ (*callsign*) is fully _____ on the ILS, runway _____

TWR: (*callsign*) report _____ outer _____. QFE _____ wind _____ _____ knots

ACFT: _____ passing _____ _____ QFE _____ (*callsign*)

(*later*)

ACFT: _____ _____ (*callsign*)

TWR: (*callsign*) continue _____, number 2 to _____

ACFT: _____ approach (*callsign*)

TWR: (*callsign*) cleared to _____

ACFT: _____ _____ _____ (*callsign*)

TWR: (*callsign*) (*landing-time*). Take first right and _____ Ground on 121.8 when _____

Boeing 747 landing at Narita Airport

10.3 TAXI INSTRUCTIONS AFTER LANDING

Listen to this

1) ACFT: Narita Ground Cathay 50 runway vacated
   GRD: Cathay 50 turn left onto taxiway A4, proceed to P3, parking stand 31
   ACFT: Via A4 to P3, stand 31 Cathay 50

2) ACFT: Narita Ground Japanair 426 request backtrack
   GRD: Japanair 426 backtrack the runway, exit A4 and hold at intersection P3
   ACFT: Backtrack exit A4 and hold at intersection P3

---

expedite vacating runway — leave runway quickly
green lights — lights marking centre of taxiway
Thai Inter — callsign for Thai International: Thai national airline
to backtrack — aircraft makes 180° turn and taxis back towards threshold of
          runway
apron management service — directs movement on apron

Boeing 747B taxiing after landing

Ex. 1   Role-play in pairs

You are the ground controller at a large international airport. Pass the instructions below to the aircraft as they contact ground control. The pilot of the aircraft acknowledges. Only 'backtrack' and 'crossing runway' instructions should be readback.

GRD:

> Turn right onto taxiway A4, follow the green lights to P4, stand 24
> Expedite vacating runway at A4 and hold at intersection P4
> Report before crossing P3
> Turn left onto taxiway A1, via A6 to P6, stand 33
> Continue to end of runway, exit A9, parking stand 405
> Follow the 747 on P6 your stand is 35
> Stop. Give way to DC-8 entering taxiway A5
> Cross runway 16, report vacated

ACFT: Ground (*callsign*) . . .

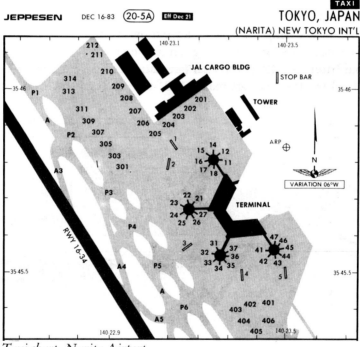

Taxi chart, Narita Airport

Ex. 2   In pairs, using the taxi chart above, guide the three aircraft below to their parking stands.

aircraft	stand
TWA 616	15
Air India 770	25
Thai Inter 009	35

10.4 MISSED APPROACH

Listen to this

1) ACFT: Tower Korean 001 outer marker
   TWR: Korean 001 runway is blocked. Go around immediately, I say again,
           go around
   ACFT: Korean 001 going around
   TWR: Korean 001 climb straight ahead to 3000 feet QNH 1009 and contact
           Approach on 125.8
   ACFT: Korean 001 3000 feet, contact Approach 125.8

2) ACFT: Thai Inter 900 outer marker
   TWR: Thai Inter 900 cleared to land. RVR 600 metres
   ACFT: Cleared to land Thai Inter 900
   ACFT: Thai Inter is going around
   TWR: Thai Inter 900 climb straight ahead to 6000 feet QNH 1010, contact
           Approach 125.8
   ACFT: Straight ahead to 6000 feet. Contact 125.8
   ACFT: Narita Approach Thai Inter 900 is going around
   APP: Thai Inter 900 hold at Martin. Report reaching
   ACFT: Holding at Martin Thai Inter 900

> **to go around** — when a pilot has to abandon his approach to land, he will climb
> in order to make a new approach or fly to an alternate airfield
> **missed approach** — when a pilot cannot complete his approach to land, usually
> due to lack of visual contact with the runway

Ex. 1   Look at the drawings below. Each one shows a situation at an airfield which might cause
a pilot to abandon his approach to land. In pairs, complete the dialogues.

Example ACFT: *Tower G-ALLF outer marker*
            TWR: *G-ALLF runway blocked due to debris, go around. Climb to 6000*
                    feet QNH 980 and contact Tower on 118.6
            ACFT: *Tower G-LF is going around*

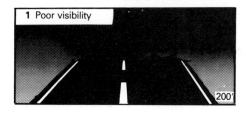

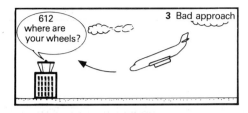

1) ACFT: Tower (*callsign*) outer marker
   TWR: (*callsign*) RVR less than 500 metres
   ACFT: ....

2) ACFT: Tower (*callsign*) outer marker
   TWR: (*callsign*) runway is...
   ACFT: ....

3) ACFT: Tower (*callsign*) going around due to ....
   TWR: (*callsign*)...
   ACFT: ....

4) ACFT: Tower (*callsign*) outer marker. Traffic ....
   TWR: (*callsign*)...
   ACFT: ....

10.5 DIVERSIONS

Listen to this

1) ACFT: Narita Approach Clipper 416 holding. Request expected approach time
   APP: Clipper 416 your EAT will not be for at least 2 hours due to blocked runway. Report intentions
   ACFT: Narita Approach understand no approach for minimum of 2 hours. Standby Clipper 416
   APP: Clipper 416 correct, standing by Narita Approach
   ACFT: Narita Approach Clipper 416 unable to hold for more than 1 hour. Request diversion to Nagoya

2) APP: TWA 108 Narita Approach aerodrome closed for snow clearance. Hold at Martin. EAT 09 00
   ACFT: Roger Approach. TWA 108 holding at Martin. Unable to hold for more than 45 minutes. Request diversion to Haneda
   APP: TWA 108 standby for further clearance
   ACFT: Standing by TWA 108

---

to divert — to change aircraft's destination
Nagoya — city in central Japan
Haneda — Tokyo's airport for domestic traffic
EAT — Estimated Approach Time, usually given by Controller when an aircraft is holding before approach

Ex. 1   There are many reasons why an aircraft would be diverted to another airfield, for example

1) bad weather conditions
2) runway closure
3) problems at the airport (strikes)
4) technical problems with the aircraft (runway may be too short if the plane has a problem with its brakes)
5) traffic congestion in the TMA

In groups of three, using the approach chart below, request diversion or advise aircraft to divert for one of the above reasons.

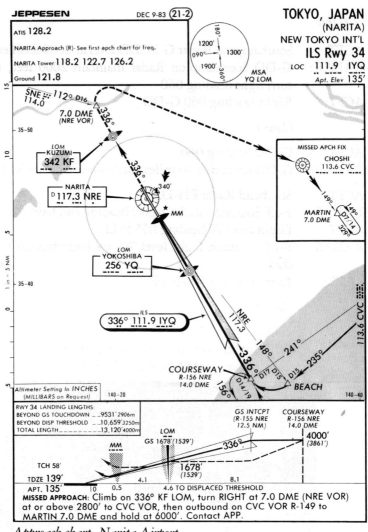

Approach chart, Narita Airport

Unit 11

Radar Phraseology

Identification   Provision of Service with Surveillance Radar
Radar Vectoring to Final Approach   Loss of Communication—Aircraft Radio Failure

11.1 IDENTIFICATION

Listen to this

1) ACFT: Southampton Radar G-BCDD level at 2000 feet heading 030
   RADAR: G-DD Southampton Radar maintain 2000 feet, for identification turn right heading 060
   ACFT: Right heading 060 G-DD

   (*later*)

   ACFT: G-DD heading 060
   RADAR: G-DD identified 10 miles south-west of the airfield

2) ACFT: Southend Radar PH-LLF
   RADAR: P-LF Southend Radar report heading and level
   ACFT: Flight level 70 heading 055 P-LF
   RADAR: P-LF maintain flight level 70, for identification turn right heading 090
   ACFT: Right heading 090 P-LF

   (*later*)

   ACFT: P-LF heading 090
   RADAR: P-LF not observed on radar, resume own navigation and standby
   ACFT: Turning back onto heading 055 resuming own navigation P-LF

Approach Radar Control

111

Southampton — airfield on south coast of England
Southend — airfield on south-east coast of England
Radar — callsign for radar controller
for identification — the controller wants to confirm the identity of the 'blip' on his radar screen (when secondary surveillance radar, SSR, is unavailable)
identified — the controller knows which 'blip' on his radar screen is the aircraft he is talking to
PH-LLF — Dutch registration
OO-RPP — Belgian registration
not identified — the controller cannot see which 'blip', if any, is turning
observed — seen
outside radar cover — outside range of radar (distance or altitude)
resume — begin again
Blackpool — airfield on north-west coast of England
Edinburgh — airfield in south-east Scotland

BAe 146

As a radar screen may have many 'blips' on it at any one time, it is sometimes difficult for a controller to tell which 'blip' he is talking to. So he will ask the pilot to 'turn' or use his identification switch on the aircraft's radar equipment.

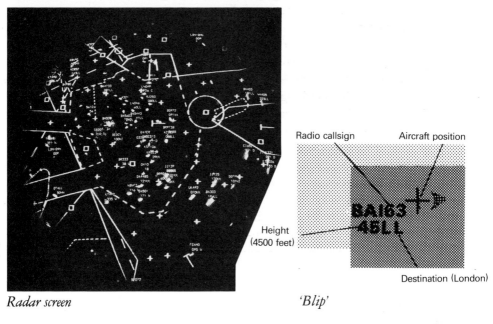

Radar screen   *'Blip'*

Radio callsign   Aircraft position

Height
(4500 feet)

Destination (London)

BA163
45LL

Ex. 1   Two aircraft are en route to an airfield in Scotland. Contact the radar controller and complete the conversations below:

1) ACFT: Blackpool Radar OO-RPP
   RADAR: Report ....
   ACFT: Level at 5000 feet heading 350 O-PP
   RADAR: O-PP...
   ACFT: Turning left heading 020 O-PP

   (later)

   ACFT: O-PP...
   RADAR: O-PP..................................... 15 miles south of airfield

2) ACFT: Edinburgh Radar D-LAMN. Level at 3000 feet. Heading 270.
   RADAR: D-LAMN Edinburgh Radar ....
              ....
   ACFT: D-MN turn right heading 300

   (later)

   ACFT: D-MN ....
   RADAR: D-MN not .... Resume own navigation
   ACFT: .... D-MN

11.2 PROVISION OF SERVICE WITH SURVEILLANCE RADAR ————

Listen to this

1) RADAR: G-DD identified 10 miles south-west of airfield. Vectoring for Visual Approach runway 21

   ACFT: Roger G-DD runway 21

2) RADAR: O-PP identified 8 miles east of airfield. This will be a Surveillance Radar Approach runway 21 terminating at 2 miles from touchdown, Obstacle Clearance Height is 500 feet. Check your minima

   ACFT: Surveillance Radar Approach runway 21 O-PP

3) RADAR: D-MN be advised ILS Approach not available due to equipment failure. Vectoring for a Surveillance Radar Approach runway 28 terminating at half mile from touchdown. Obstacle Clearance Height is 350 feet. Check your minima

   ACFT: Roger ILS not available. Vectoring for Surveillance Radar Approach runway 28 D-MN

Surveillance Radar Approach (SRA) — radar controller uses primary or secondary radar to vector an aircraft (see diagram on page 115)

to terminate — to stop

Obstacle Clearance Height (OCH) — height above airfield or runway threshold for a particular approach route, below which an aircraft may collide with obstacles

minima — the operating company often has a higher level for Obstacle Clearance Height

equipment failure — equipment not working

Obstacle Clearance Altitude (OCA) — height above mean sea level for a particular approach route, below which an aircraft may collide with obstacles

---

Sometimes a pilot will be on approach to an airfield which has no Instrument Landing System or where this system is unserviceable. However, if there is primary or secondary radar equipment installed, the radar controller will be able to give the pilot radar vectors to within half a mile, or two miles of the threshold, but only if he is trained and licensed for SRAs.

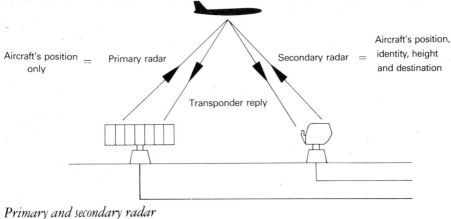

Primary and secondary radar

||||||||||||||||||||||||||||||||||||||||||||||||||||||||||||||||||||||||||||||||||||||||||||||

Ex. 1   Instruct the pilot of the aircraft you have just identified that you will be providing him with a certain type of radar service on Final Approach. Use the ideas below:

> visual
> ILS
> SRA

> runway
> instructions terminate at . . . mile(s)
> OCH or OCA

Boeing 757

11.3 RADAR VECTORING TO FINAL APPROACH

Listen to this

1) RADAR: G-DD turn right heading 040, descend to 1500 feet QFE 998 wind 250° 15 knots

   ACFT: Heading 040 leaving 2000 feet for 1500 feet QFE 998 G-DD

   RADAR: G-DD continue on heading. You are right-hand downwind for runway 21. Will you accept a 6-mile final?

2) RADAR: G-DD turn right heading 150 check wheels

   ACFT: Wheels down. Heading 150 G-DD

   RADAR: G-DD to intercept the centreline runway 21, turn right heading 190 closing from the right

   ACFT: Right heading 190 G-DD

   RADAR: G-DD turn right heading 215 final approach

   ACFT: Right heading 215 G-DD

3) RADAR: G-DD on final approach track, heading is good. 7 miles from touchdown . . . Left of track, turn right 5° heading 220 . . . 5 miles from touchdown. Commence descent now to maintain a 3° glide path. Cleared to land runway 21 wind 190° 10 knots

   ACFT: Cleared to land runway 21 G-DD

---

wheels down (and locked) — landing equipment is down and locked into position

track — path to touchdown (see diagram on page 117)

approach completed — no further instructions will be given

heading is good — correct heading

centreline — approach track centreline

Ex. 1   Listen to a radar controller guiding an aircraft to within sight of the runway. Then answer these questions:

1) At a range of 4 miles the height should be
   a) 1500 feet?
   b) 1450 feet?
   c) 450 feet?
   d) 1250 feet?

2) Was the aircraft
   a) right of centreline?
   b) on track?
   c) left of centreline?

3) After turning left 5° was the heading
   a) 205?
   b) 125?
   c) 315?
   d) 215?

4) When the approach was completed, was the range from touchdown
   a) 1½ miles?
   b) ½ mile?
   c) 2 miles?
   d) 1 mile?

(Text of tape and answers in Appendix 3)

Radar vectoring to final approach

Ex. 2   G-CFBO is at 1500 feet QFE and the controller has already vectored the aircraft to intercept the final approach track of runway 26 at 8 nautical miles from touchdown, for a 2 nautical miles SRA. In pairs, complete the pilot's part of the transmission and fill in the missing words.

RADAR: G-BO turn right heading 260 _____ Approach
ACFT: ....
RADAR: G-BO _____ 8 miles
ACFT: ....
RADAR: G-BO _____ of track. Turn right 5° heading 265
ACFT: ....
RADAR: G-BO range 7 miles from _____
ACFT: ....
RADAR: G-BO range 6 miles. _____ wheels and _____
ACFT: ....
RADAR: G-BO approaching 5 miles. _____ descent
   _____ to maintain a 3° glide path QFE 1008
RADAR: G-BO 4½ miles _____ _____. Height
   _____ _____ 1350 feet

ACFT: ....
RADAR: G-BO 4 miles _____ _____. _____
   _____ be 1200 feet. Cleared to land runway 26.

_____ 260° 10 knots. 3 miles _____

_____.   _____   _____

900 feet. Check your _____. G-BO 2 miles _____

_____.   _____   _____

600 feet. Approach _____. Out

Long range civil radar, Sunsvall, Sweden

11.4 LOSS OF COMMUNICATION — AIRCRAFT RADIO FAILURE —

Listen to this

If the controller loses radio contact with an aircraft or thinks he might have lost it, he can transmit certain instructions to see if he can be heard.

1) RADAR: G-BO radio contact lost. If you read, squawk ident, I say again squawk ident

   RADAR: G-BO squawk observed. Will continue to pass instructions

2) RADAR: G-BO reply not received. Turn left heading 150, I say again turn left heading 150

   RADAR: G-BO turn observed. Will continue to pass instructions

Ex. 1   Complete the radar controller's messages.

1) RADAR: G-LO if you read .... (*turn*)
   RADAR: G-LO ....

2) RADAR: G-HM radio contact lost............................... (*squawk*)
   RADAR: G-HM ....

3) RADAR: Reply not received.. (*turn*)
   RADAR: ....

Unit 12

Distress and Urgency Messages

Distress Messages and Acknowledgement
Imposition and Cancellation of Silence Condition and Distress Communications
Transfer of other Aircraft to Another Frequency
Urgency Messages and Acknowledgements   Emergency Descent

12.1 DISTRESS MESSAGES AND ACKNOWLEDGEMENT

Listen to this

1) ACFT: MAYDAY MAYDAY MAYDAY Le Touquet Tower G-BYCM DC-3 port engine on fire. Position 6 miles south of Le Touquet, 3000 feet, losing altitude. Heading 010. Request straight-in approach to Le Touquet

   TWR: G-BYCM Le Touquet Tower roger MAYDAY

2) ACFT: MAYDAY MAYDAY MAYDAY London Control F-AACV Cessna 310 fuel emergency. Ditching in sea. Position 30 miles west of Land's End. Flight level 100 heading 090, speed 160 knots, 3 persons on board

   ACC: F-AACV London Control roger MAYDAY out

Emergency Controllers in the Distress and Diversion Cell

3) ACFT: MAYDAY MAYDAY MAYDAY Manston Tower D-AXFB Piper
            Cherokee from Hamburg. I'm unsure of my position. Endurance 15
            minutes. Request radar vectoring to Manston D-AXFB

   TWR: D-AXFB Manston Tower roger MAYDAY

The Distress Signal is the word 'MAYDAY' — this signal is only used when an aircraft
needs immediate assistance. 'MAYDAY' should be spoken three times.

In order to help you, the following points, or as many as possible, should be included in
a distress message:

1) MAYDAY call
2) Callsign and aircraft type
3) Type of emergency, for example, engine failure
4) Position
5) Altitude
6) Heading
7) Intentions, for example, ditching
8) Speed
9) Number of people on board

MAYDAY — distress signal

port — on the left side of the aircraft

starboard — on the right side of the aircraft

London Control Distress and Diversion Cell (D and D Cell) — Answers
            distress calls on 121.5 MHz (VHF) or 243.0 MHz (UHF) and
            informs nearest airfield of the aircraft in distress

ditching — to land aircraft on water surface, for example, sea, river, lake

I'm unsure of my position — the pilot is lost

Advisory Route — a type of airway where an Air Traffic Service (ATS) is provided
            but safe separation from other aircraft cannot be guaranteed

report status — report any changes in distress situation

squawk 7700 — emergency transponder code

to extinguish a fire — to put out a fire

Ex. 1   In pairs, call up London Control. Only give distress signal, callsign, type of aircraft and type of emergency, using the information in the boxes below.

Example   *ACFT:*   MAYDAY   MAYDAY   MAYDAY   *London Control G-FLOD One-Eleven port engine on fire, unable to extinguish*
           ACC: *G-FLOD London Control roger MAYDAY*

> **callsign**
> G-XAOL
> D-AAST
> HB-IHA
> F-LLAX

> **emergency situation**
> engine(s) on fire
> engine failure (port/starboard)
> cabin fire
> lost in fog/bad weather
> fuel emergency
> explosion
> collision/bird strike
> action by hostile aircraft

aircraft

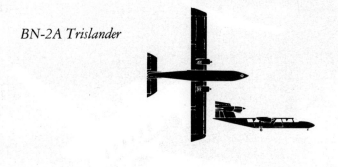

BN-2A Trislander

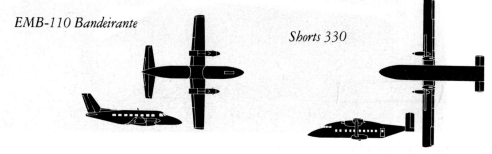

EMB-110 Bandeirante

Shorts 330

Ex. 2   Keep calm!

Remember, a controller should use a calm, clear, confident voice, and, in an emergency, only ask for one piece of information at a time.

In pairs, using the situations below, ask the pilot questions in order to find out relevant facts.

---

information wanted
number of persons on board — aircraft type — heading — position — altitude — speed — transponder — endurance — alternate — intentions

---

Emergency (1) — Cessna Citation from Edinburgh to Aberdeen 10 persons on board. Transponder, 5000 feet, heading 075, 15 miles north of airfield, speed 180 knots

Emergency (2) — Piper Aztec VFR from Lille to Brussels 2 persons on board. No transponder, heading 030, 3000 feet 10 miles north-west of Lille

Example   *CONTROL:*   *Report heading*
              ACFT: *030 F-LLAX*

Cessna Citation III

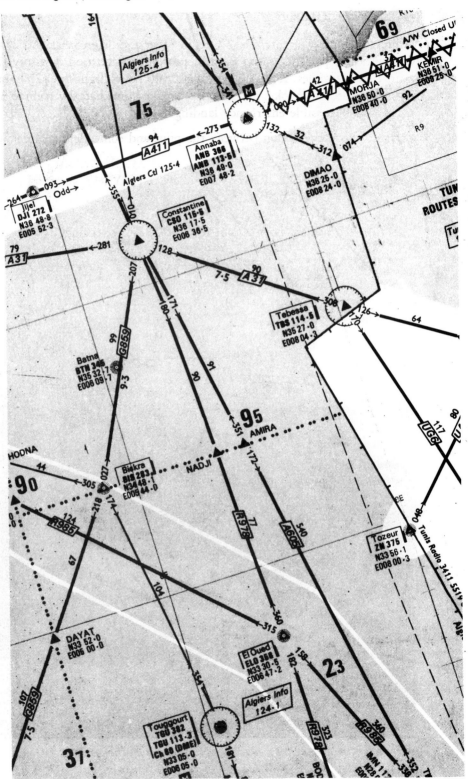

Section of high altitude chart, North Africa

Ex. 3   **Trouble over Algeria!**

An aircraft, south of Constantine VOR, in Algeria, callsign Sahara Air 251, a Boeing 707, with 200 passengers and 8 crew, proceeding north on Advisory Route 859, destination Marseilles. It passed Biskra at 0800 hours flight level 250 heading 027. Severe cabin fire and smoke. Pilot wishes to make immediate diversion to Algiers, but warns ATC of possible emergency landing.

Complete this conversation between the pilot and controller at Algiers Control:

ACFT: ....

ACC: Sahara Air 251 Algiers Control roger MAYDAY go ahead

ACFT: ....

ACC: Roger MAYDAY Sahara Air 251 squawk 7700 ident. Turn left heading 330 and descend to flight level 100. Report change in status

ACFT: ....

ACC: Roger 251. Immediate emergency landing. Identified 30 miles north of Biskra, QNH 1030 wind reported as 230° 25 knots

ACFT: ....

Airport firemen putting out a simulated fire during a practice session

12.2 IMPOSITION AND CANCELLATION OF SILENCE CONDITIONS AND DISTRESS COMMUNICATIONS

Imposition of Silence Condition

After a ground station receives a call from an aircraft in distress, it may tell all other stations and aircraft in the area, or one particular aircraft, to be silent so that they do not interfere with the distress call.

Listen to this

1) TWR: All stations, Barcelona Tower, stop transmitting, MAYDAY
2) ACC: D-BIXT, stop transmitting, MAYDAY Bremen Control out

> **Barcelona Tower** — control tower at Barcelona airport, in Spain
> **Bremen Control** — ACC in West Germany
> **to cancel a distress call** — emergency is finished
> **Distress Traffic Ended** — aircraft is not in danger any longer
> **Orly** — airport near Paris
> **Oslo Tower** — control tower at Oslo airport, in Norway
> **Maastricht Control** — Upper Air Control Centre for Northern Europe

Ex. 1   You are a controller at an ATSU. Instruct the following to be silent:

ACC:	All Stations F-CAFT I-ARCO HB-AVL	Orly Tower Oslo Tower Maastricht Control	stop transmitting, MAYDAY

Cancellation of Distress Communication and of Silence Condition

When the emergency is over and the aircraft is no longer in distress, it transmits a message cancelling the distress condition. The ground station will then cancel the silence condition.

Listen to this

1) ACFT: MAYDAY Barcelona Tower G-DX cancel distress. Engine re-started. Returning to Barcelona

   TWR: MAYDAY G-DX Barcelona Tower understand cancel distress. All stations, Barcelona Tower 1530 hours. G-ACDX distress traffic ended, out

2) ACFT: MAYDAY Bremen Control D-XT cancel distress. Fire in cabin extinguished. Maintaining altitude, request clearance to Bremen

ACC: MAYDAY D-XT Bremen Control understand cancel distress. Cleared to approach, contact Bremen Radar on 124.5. All stations Bremen Control 09 15 hours, D-BIXT distress traffic ended, out

Ex. 2 In pairs, using the information below, cancel your distress call and inform the ground station of your intentions. Acknowledge cancellation and cancel the silence condition. Make up a callsign for your aircraft.

Example *ACFT:* *MAYDAY Brussels Tower F-LD cancel distress. Engine restarted. Proceeding to Amsterdam*

TWR: *MAYDAY F-LD understand cancel distress. All stations Brussels Tower 16 00 hours, F-MCLD distress traffic ended, out*

Tower/ACC	event	intentions
Brussels Tower	engine re-started	Proceeding to . . .
Barcelona Control	fire extinguished	Request diversion . . .
Stuttgart Tower	position established	Request joining and landing
Amsterdam Radar	hostile aircraft	instructions
Vienna Tower	departed	Flight continuing
	airframe icing	Request clearance to
	problem cancelled	rejoin airway

Extinguishing a fire using chemical foam

12.3 TRANSFER OF OTHER AIRCRAFT TO ANOTHER FREQUENCY —

The ground station which answers the distress call may decide to advise other aircraft to change to another frequency.

Listen to this

1) TWR: MAYDAY EC-CCE all other aircraft contact Tenerife Tower on 118.7
2) TWR: I-DIKX contact Torino Tower on 118.2. If negative contact, return to this frequency

Ex. 1   You are a controller at an ATSU. Instruct other traffic to transfer to another frequency. Complete the instructions below.

Example *ATSU: MAYDAY HB-LFX contact Geneva Tower on 118.7*

ATSU:	MAYDAY	*(callsign)* all other aircraft	contact _____ on _____

ATSU
Lisbon Tower
France Control
Dublin Control
Prestwick Tower
Malaga Tower

frequencies
118.2
120.5
122.8
118.3
119.4

12.4 URGENCY MESSAGES AND ACKNOWLEDGEMENTS ——————

Listen to this

1) ACFT: PAN PAN PAN Biggin Hill G-CEPT Cessna 340 one passenger severely ill. 15 miles south of airfield at 3000 feet heading 340, IMC. Request immediate joining instructions and medical assistance on landing
   TWR: G-CEPT Biggin Hill roger PAN. Join downwind for runway 01

2) ACFT: PAN PAN PAN Gatwick Approach Air Portugal 475 Boeing 737 50 passengers 5 crew. Number 1 engine shutdown, 15 miles out 5000 feet QNH

APP: Air Portugal 475 Gatwick Approach roger PAN. Continue approach. Contact Tower 118.5. Emergency services alerted, out

The urgency signal is the word 'PAN'. An aircraft transmitting an urgency message is usually not in immediate danger. A single-engined light aircraft with a power failure sends a MAYDAY call. However, a Hercules with one engine failed might send a PAN, but would not send a MAYDAY. PAN messages are not used very often.

Biggin Hill — airfield in south-east England
shutdown — power failure
to alert — to warn
emergency services — for example, fire engines, foam carpet, ambulances
carburettor icing — when the carburettor ices up, the engine loses power
airframe icing — ice on wings and fuselage may affect aircraft's handling
lose control of pitch — be unable to stop aircraft's nose going up and down
QDM — magnetic heading to steer the aircraft to the ground station
to transmit for DF — the pilot usually transmits a few words so that the ground can give the aircraft a magnetic heading to fly
rating — for example, Private Pilot (PPL with IMC) (Instrument Meteorological Conditions)
Le Bourget — airfield north of Paris
cold front — cold air

Cessna 150

Ex. 1   You are a (student) pilot flying a Cessna 150 VFR. Choose one of the following situations and send a PAN message, giving the necessary information.

Example *ACFT:*   *PAN PAN PAN Le Bourget Tower G-ABCD PPL. I am ill. 8 miles north of airfield 2000 feet QNH descending heading 160. Request joining instructions*

ACFT:	PAN PAN PAN	*(ATSU)*	*(callsign)*	I am ill. Instructor ill. Fuel shortage. Passenger ill.

(Position)	*(Altitude)*	*(Heading)*	*(Intentions)*

Ex. 2   In pairs, complete the conversations below between a pilot and a controller.

1) You are a PPL in a single-engined aircraft from Le Touquet to Le Bourget. Fifteen minutes after departure you fly into a cold front. You experience carburettor icing and airframe icing. You start to lose control of pitch and direction.

ACFT: _____ _____ _____ Le Touquet
           G-BCDO Cessna 150 departed _____ 15 minutes ago.
           Having difficulty in _____ _____ south of your
           _____. Request QDMs back to _____ urgently
TWR: Roger PAN _____. Transmit for _____
ACFT: G_____ one, two, three, two, one _____

2) You are the pilot of a Piper Cherokee with two passengers, en route for Orly, Paris from Biggin Hill. Nearing the French coast, you begin to experience severe turbulence and icing problems.

ACFT: PAN PAN PAN Le Touquet Tower G-ABCO Piper Cherokee 3 p.o.b.
           Due _____ _____ request immediate
           _____ and _____ instructions. 5 miles
           _____ of _____ at 2000 feet _____
           heading 140 PPL with IMC
TWR: G-ABCO _____ _____ roger _____.
           _____ to circuit height 1000 feet QFE 1008 and
           _____ base leg

(Answers in Appendix 3)

12.5 EMERGENCY DESCENT

Listen to this

1) ACFT: MAYDAY MAYDAY MAYDAY Shanwick Control TWA 100 be advised of emergency descent position 51° 05′ N 043° 07′ W, descending from flight level 370 to flight level 150

2) ACFT: MAYDAY MAYDAY MAYDAY London Control Speedbird 505 be advised of emergency descent position 5 DME south of Daventry VOR, descending from flight level 270 to flight level 120

3) ATSU: London Control emergency to all concerned. Emergency descent 5 miles south of Daventry VOR. All aircraft below flight level 270 within 30 miles of Daventry VOR maintain heading and altitude

Sometimes it is necessary for an aircraft to make an emergency descent to a lower level. This is generally due to sudden decompression. The ground station which the aircraft in difficulty has called will then warn other traffic in the area.

Ex. 1 Imagine you are a controller who has just received a message from an aircraft making an emergency descent. Alert other traffic in the vicinity:

ATSU: (*ATSU*) emergency to all concerned. Emergency _____ miles _____ of X-ray VOR. All aircraft below flight level _____ within _____ miles of X-ray VOR _____ heading and altitude

Ex. 2 Going Down!

You are the pilot of an airliner which has just departed from Lisbon West International Airport, destination Caracas, Venezuela. Thirty minutes after departure, at flight level 330, the aircraft experiences depressurisation, i.e. the pressure in the aircraft drops. Send a MAYDAY signal and inform the ACC that you are making an emergency descent. Complete the following conversation:

ACFT (1): MAYDAY MAYDAY MAYDAY Lisbon West, Argentina 002 emergency descent

ACC: ....

ACFT (1): Argentina 002 depressurised flight level 330. Descending rapidly heading 180, approaching Narta reporting point

ACC: Argentina 002 roger MAYDAY, call when level. BREAK, BREAK. Clipper 420 conflicting emergency traffic 12 o'clock 15 miles. Turn left immediately heading 360 and _____ _____ flight level 220

ACFT (2):   Clipper 420 turning left heading 360. Say again flight level

ACC: _____ _____ flight level _____

Lisbon West

ACFT (2):   Roger flight level 220 Clipper 420

(*Answers in Appendix 3*)

CONSOLIDATION

It is for the pilot to assess the situation and send either a MAYDAY or PAN signal. From the list below of different distress and urgency situations, send and acknowledge MAYDAY or PAN messages, giving as much information as you can. Work in pairs, one as the pilot of the aircraft, the other as the controller.

emergencies
fire and/or smoke
airframe icing in a light aircraft
unsure of position
fuel emergency
sudden depressurisation
engine(s) failure

urgency
undercarriage failure
tyre burst
crew/passenger ill
engine(s) failure
electrical/instrument failure

Appendix 1

Examples of Non-standard Phraseology

BAC One-Eleven

These dialogues are not recorded.

The phrases in italics represent non-standard examples of radiotelephony phraseology. The standard phraseology, or the meaning of these phrases, is given in bold type after each dialogue. It is very important to remember that you should never use these non-standard phrases yourself. Examples are given here so that if you hear them, you will know what they mean.

Note
Imaginary callsigns are used for aircraft or ATSUs. Words in brackets are unnecessary.

BASIC OPERATING PROCEDURES

1) ACFT: _____ Approach, *good morning* Swallow 401
   APP: *Good morning* Swallow 401

   You may also hear '*good evening*', '*good night*', '*good day*', '*bye*', '*cheerio*'.

2) ACFT: _____ Control, Air Everest 103 747 heavy
   ACC: *Sorry* say again *calling?*

   say again callsign

   ACFT: _____ Control Air Everest 103
   ACC: Roger, Air Everest 103. *You're rather weak**. (Can you) *call 121.8***

   *readability 2
   **contact 121.8

3) ACFT: Liberty Tower Texas 801 *is with you*

   on your frequency

4) ACFT: _____ Tower G-AZFL *on frequency*

   on your frequency

5) TWR: N-5TX change to *1211*
   121.1

6) TWR: New World 678 contact Tower *2525*
   125.25

7) TWR: Pasta 610 first left, turn left Whisky ground *9*
   121.9

8) RADAR: Contact _____ Control 129 decimal 0
   ACFT: Sun 1801 *with* _____ *Control** 129 *point*** 0, *goodbye!*

   *on your frequency
   **decimal

9) ATSU: G-ABCD *listen out* Tower

   monitor Tower

AERODROME INFORMATION

1) ACFT: Tower Kilt 676 *I'd like a** visibility check
   TOWER: *In excess of*** 1500 metres touchdown, 1400 midpoint, 1500 stop end

   *request visibility
   **more than 1500m touchdown

2) ACFT: Ground Kilt 254 confirm C is closed
   GROUND: Correct. C is closed to DC-10s due to the work in progress
   ACFT: *And B is closed as well, isn't it?**
   GROUND: Negative. B is open now
   ACFT: *OK 254***

   *Is B closed?
   **Roger, Kilt 254
   (C and B are taxiways)

3) TWR: Alpine 493 clear to land 33. Wind is 280° 7 kilometres per hour. Runway is wet and water *pools** *up to*** 2 millimetres

   *patches
   **depth

SURFACE MOVEMENT AND TAKE-OFF

1) TWR: Swallow 726 (just) confirm (that) callsign
   ACFT: Swallow 726
   TWR: 726 roger. *You're clear to start** when ready *to make*** your on the hour slot for Frankfurt. Your clearance is a Dover One F Departure squawking 5363

   *start-up approved
   **to be in time for

2) ACFT: Lion 774 push-back *B4**
   GROUND: Lion 774 is cleared to *push***

   *request push-back from stand B4
   **push-back approved

3) ACFT: Shuttle 8M *to taxi**
   GROUND: Shuttle 8M on the *inner*** taxiway, holding point 28 right
   ACFT: *Inner*** (for) 28R, Shuttle 8M

   *request taxi clearance
   **give taxiway letter e.g. P or A

4) ACFT: Lion 774 *can we nip on to the outer** to get past Olympic?
    GROUND: Affirmative. (Just about to call you.) Switch on to the *outer***,
                work in progress

*can we go on to taxiway **B** to pass aircraft in front of us?
**give taxiway letter

5) GROUND: New World 760 your *parking M33**, north on the *inner*** taxiway
    ACFT: *On the blocks*† at 45. 760

*your stand is **M33**
**give taxiway letter
†stand

6) TOWER: Lion 774 (can you just) hold position (there). *I've got one in a tight
                box to get away from the full length*
    ACFT: 774 holding

the slot-time of this aircraft is nearly finished and the aircraft needs the
complete runway to take off.

7) TOWER: Marathon 262 *take** a left turn and *line up (and hold)*** on 28 right
*make
**line up and wait

8) TOWER: Marathon 262 (cleared for) take-off 28 right. The wind is 230° at 10
                knots, *call rolling*
    ACFT: Cleared to go

report departing

9) TOWER: Castle 069 in the *holding area**, hold on the left-hand side, I'll call
                you *shortly***

*holding point/holding bay
**very soon

10) TOWER: Tiger 10 hold at the top end of 23. *I'll give you** line up clearance
                *shortly***

*expect
**very soon

11) TOWER: Castle 069 clear to line up (and hold) runway 28 right. (There
                will be) *one departing from further down the runway before you*

one ahead to depart

DEPARTING FLIGHTS AND FLIGHT INFORMATION SERVICE

1) TOWER: Queen 725 Turn left heading 110, *cleared to 4000* QNH 1024
   climb to 4000 feet

2) TOWER: Queen 725 contact *Director* 120.4
   (controller in) **Approach** (Radar Control) (= Arrival)

3) RADAR: Kilt 943 *maintain a good rate of climb through 100 to 120*
   expedite climb until flight level 120

4) FIS: N2-TC *what's the ride like?*
   report flight conditions

5) ACC: Snow 531 Squawk 5432 *set course towards* Clacton
   set heading for

EN ROUTE INSTRUCTIONS

1) RADAR: OD-4012 Further climb *shortly**, *there's traffic crossing in front of you***
   *very soon
   **traffic crossing ahead from left to right/right to left

2) RADAR: King 413 *route direct to Worthing*, (your) track approximately 165°
   cleared to Worthing direct or proceed direct to Worthing

3) ACFT: Sunline 113 *out of* flight level 90 for flight level 70
   leaving

4) ACFT: *We'd like to climb out of cloud because we've got engine and icing problems**
             Air Ruby 511
   RADAR: Roger. *I'll (just) check*** with (the) next sector. Standby . . . Air
             Ruby 511 *you are now cleared†* to flight level 200
   *request climb due to engine and icing problem
   **confirming level change
   †climb

5) RADAR: Air Everest 195 $\begin{bmatrix} \textit{Can you accept flight level 310} \\ \textit{Could you take flight level 310} \end{bmatrix}$ at this time?
   Can you climb to flight level 310 now?

6) ACFT: Radar OD-2056 *We will be looking for 350 later*
   RADAR: Roger 2056, standby for further clearance
   request climb to flight level 350

7) ACFT: _____ Control Beach 515 *just coming up to* Abbeville
    approaching

8) ATSU: Union 008 *you're (? your) passing level now?*
    report level

9) ACFT: _____ Control OD 440 *we are looking for descent now*
    request immediate descent clearance

10) ACC: Cheese 770 *continue your left turn and roll-out direct to Eastwood*
    left turn and leave for Eastwood direct

HOLDING — APPROACH — LANDING

1) ACC: Sun 1130 *route direct to Ibsley to take up the hold*
    direct to Ibsley to enter the hold

2) ACC: Sun 1130. *Next time round to Ibsley*, make it inbound 010 with a right
    turn***

    *at Ibsley
    **right turn inbound heading 010

3) ACC: Blue Line 808 *I'll be running you west for a little while*, then turning you
    back downwind***

    *heading 270 until further instructed
    **turn downwind

4) APP: Castle 069 *come back on the speed a bit*
    reduce your speed

5) ACFT: OD-540 we have good ground contact. *Can we continue on visual?*
    request visual approach

6) ACFT: TOWER G-ABCD *overshooting*
    going around

7) TWR: Snow 700 *do you receive the localiser off on your right?*
    report established on the localiser

8) TWR: Snow 700 *on the ground* 57
    landing time

9) TWR: Alpine 501 clear to land. *Caution wake vortex*.* Recommended spacing
    is . . . *miles***

*Turbulence generated by aircraft in flight, particularly large aircraft flying slowly. It is experienced behind and slightly below the aircraft. Its effect on a following aircraft is most dangerous at take-off and initial climb. See diagram.

**Spacing depends on size of aircraft preceding. For example, Boeing 747 followed by Piper Cherokee, approximately 15 miles.

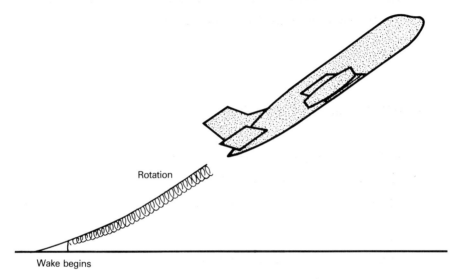

Wake vortex caused by departing aircraft

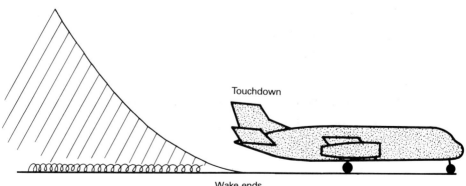

Wake vortex caused by landing aircraft

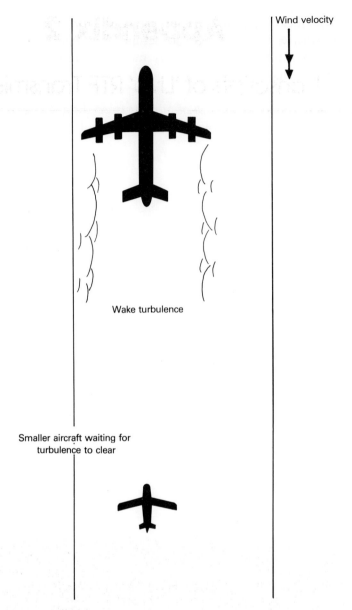

Wind velocity

Wake turbulence

Smaller aircraft waiting for
turbulence to clear

Wake turbulence caused by large aircraft

NOTE — Phonetic Alphabet

In Latin American countries, the following may be heard instead of the standard phonetic alphabet:

C — Coca
M — Metro
N — Nectar
X — Extra

Appendix 2

Transcripts of 'Live' RTF Transmissions

Boeing 737

On the tape you can hear some authentic transmissions from ATSUs in different countries. They are recorded in the same order as the transcripts printed here. These recordings will give you practice in listening to a variety of accents. They include some examples of non-standard phraseology and some examples of unusual situations which controllers may have to deal with from time to time. Where something is said in a language other than English this is indicated in brackets, for example (Spanish).

MEXICO CITY INTERNATIONAL AIRPORT

ACFT: Clearance Eastern 908
TWR: Eastern 908 go ahead
ACFT: Ground Control we were delayed here, had a little maintenance problem and Ground told me to call you back. I thought maybe you had something for me
TWR: Yes sir. Your — your Flight Plan overdue and was cancelled because proposed time was changed. So, you call your company and ask them to send us the Flight Plan again please
ACFT: OK. All we want is the same one you had before. You can't still get it back for us?
TWR: That is not possible to do that. Because once we cancel the Flight Plan, it disappears from here, so we have to ask for another one by the inter-communicator
ACFT: How long does that take?
TWR: As soon as they send the Flight Plan
ACFT: OK

  (*later*)

ACFT: Mexico Eastern 908
TWR: Yes, go ahead
ACFT: While we're waiting for our clearance we would like to be able to taxi to a position where we can do an engine run-up
TWR: Standby. I'm still looking for your Flight Plan. Standby One. (*Spanish*) OK Eastern 908, got your Flight Plan. I have your clearance
ACFT: Eastern 908 go ahead
TWR: Eastern 908 is cleared to Atlanta Airport by J19 Tampico Flight Planned Route. Flight Level 330. Squawk 7316. Make a Tepexpan One Departure
ACFT: OK. That's Atlanta J19 Tampico Flight Planned Route 330. Tepexpan One Departure. Squawk 7316
TWR: That's correct Eastern 908. When ready, contact Ground on 1219
ACFT: OK. Thank you very much

TOKYO INTERNATIONAL AIRPORT, NARITA, JAPAN

ACFT: Clipper 15 needs to turn off here and hold for a little bit, a maintenance problem
TWR: Clipper 15 understand. Hold there. How long does it take to be finished?
ACFT: Just about a few minutes
TWR: A few minutes roger. Advise late for take-off and starting taxi-up again
ACFT: OK we'll call

(later)

ACFT: OK the Clipper 15 needs to taxi back
TWR: Understand you are going to taxi back
ACFT: Yes. We need to get a change of radio
TWR: Clipper 15 understand. Taxi via A taxiway
ACFT: A taxiway
TWR: Clipper 15 contact Ground on 1218 again
ACFT: 1218

J.F. KENNEDY INTERNATIONAL AIRPORT, NEW YORK

TWR: 70K 31 right at B position hold
ACFT: 70K holding at B

(later)

TWR: 70K fly runway heading. Cleared for take-off 31 right. Traffic on a 2½ mile final
ACFT: 70K roger. Will expedite take-off

WARSAW INTERNATIONAL AIRPORT, POLAND

ACFT: Warsaw Tower Lot 514 good morning. Fully established on ILS runway 33
TWR: Good morning Lot 514. Continue ILS approach for runway 33. Report passing the outer marker inbound
ACFT: Will do
ACFT: Swissair 493 there are birds, a flock of birds on the runway 29
ACFT: 514 after passing outer marker
TWR: Swissair 493 stop rolling. Hold your position
ACFT: Roger, we are holding. We couldn't take-off because there were birds on the runway
TWR: Roger BREAK 514, you are cleared to land runway 33 wind 280 7 kilometres per hour
ACFT: We are cleared to land Lot 514

LEONARDO DA VINCI AIRPORT, ROME, ITALY

ACFT: Tower Speedbird 3 we have a dog loose on the airfield. He's just going
          between B7 and B8, crossing towards BL
TWR: Speedbird 3 say again, please
ACFT: We have a dog on the grass, just where we are now
TWR: Roger, roger, a dog, roger
ACFT: Speedbird 3 the dog is going, heading towards the JAL DC-8   *4 engine*
TWR: OK, OK
ACFT: Er, a DC-10   *3 engine*

MAIQUETIA AREA CONTROL CENTRE, CARACAS, VENEZUELA

ACFT: Maiquetia N901MH
ACC: Go ahead
ACFT: OK Sir, with you. We are cruising 120 to 350, estimating Maiquetia at 44
ACC: Estimating Maiquetia at 44? Leaving 12 thousand?
ACFT: Affirmative
ACC: OK. Squawk 5555. Estimate BELLO, AVELO — what is your route after
          Maiquetia?
ACFT: Amber 18 from Maiquetia
ACC: Amber 18. Thank you sir . . . OK, is approved flight level 350. Estimate
          AVELO 18 — 1754
ACFT: We are squawking 5555 and we're estimating BELLO at five six, fifty-six,
          1756
ACC: Roger, roger. Cleared to maintain flight level 350. Proceed after Maiquetia
          direct to BELLO position, over
ACFT: 901 wilco

AREA CONTROL CENTRE, NICOSIA, CYPRUS

ACFT: Nicosia Control Air France 140 Bonjour
ACC: Air France 140 go ahead
ACFT: From Charles de Gaulle to Beirut, passing MUT at 42, flight level 290,
          estimating VESAR at 51
ACC: Roger. Maintain 290. Report VESAR
ACFT: Maintain 290. Report over VESAR 140

KAI TAK INTERNATIONAL AIRPORT, HONG KONG

APP: Swissair 166 turn right heading 070 to intercept the localiser. Cleared for IGS approach

ACFT: Heading 070, cleared for approach Swissair 166

APP: China 3002 radar service terminated. Continue with Kwangchow

ACFT: Roger 3002, good-day

APP: Good-day sir . . . China 303 continue the IGS approach. Radar service terminated. Contact Tower on 118.7

ACFT: 1187

ACC: Good-day

ACFT: Hong Kong Departure Singapore 1 good morning

APP: Singapore 1 Hong Kong Approach good morning. Radar contact

ACFT: Thank you

ACFT: Swissair 166 is coming LT inbound and we are established

APP: Roger Swissair 166 continue the IGS approach. Radar service terminated. Contact Tower 118.7

ACFT: Good morning

APP: Good morning, sir

KAI TAK AIRPORT

ACFT: Hong Kong Tower Helicopter 54

TWR: 54 Tower go

ACFT: 54 is inbound from Cheung Chau to Green Island. Amendment to Flight Plan to proceed to Tamar, pick up three passengers — negative, five passengers for Green Island back to Cheung Chau. Over

TWR: 54 roger. Not above 500 feet, report Green Island for Tamar

ACFT: OK 54

TWR: 54 QNH now 1018

ACFT: 54

ACFT: 521 Good afternoon. Is Green Island inbound

TWR: 521 roger. Make a wide approach please. I have one departing

ACFT: 521 OK

TWR: 710 confirm is cleared to land

ACFT: 710 is cleared to land

TWR: 710 ten minutes ago the company TriStar reporting lifting windshear on short final runway 13 approximately 500 feet

ACFT: Cathay 710

ACFT: 54 seven on board requesting lift-off Tamar for Green Island and Cheung Chau

TWR: 54 affirmative. Not above 500 feet. Report Green Island

ACFT: Not above 500 feet. Will report Green Island 54

ACFT: Cathay 501 is turning right over CC
TWR: Cathay 501 Hong Kong Tower good afternoon. Continue approach.
        Report abeam Green Island. Number 1 is just passed Green Island
ACFT: Sir
TWR: 01 Two companies' aircraft have reported lifting windshear on short final
        from 500 feet down to 300 feet
ACFT: 01

DUBLIN AREA CONTROL CENTRE, DUBLIN, EIRE

ACFT: And Dublin Centre the Abbair 049 requesting descent. We are 31 miles
        out
ACC: Abbair 049 descend flight level 55
ACFT: Roger, leaving 7 for 55
ACC: Air Tours 446Q maintain 170, on reaching contact London Radar 131.05
        goodnight
ACFT: Radar London 131.05 goodnight
ACC: Aer Lingus 777 present level?
ACFT: 777 flight level 60
ACC: Roger . . . WG 926 present level?
ACFT: Level 90 now
ACC: 926 roger normal navigation. Report LIFFEY
ACFT: Normal navigation. Report LIFFEY

AUCKLAND INTERNATIONAL AIRPORT, NEW ZEALAND

TWR: Confirm DCO
ACFT: Negative DCK
TWR: DCK roger. Taxi holding runway 23 Information B 1021 millibars Time
        15 and are you VFR or IFR?
ACFT: VFR requesting 6000
TWR: Roger 6000

INTERNATIONAL AIRPORT, CAIRO, U.A.R.

TWR: WW 504 Cairo Tower
ACFT: Cairo Tower WW 504 good morning. 3 miles final for runway 34
TWR: You are in sight. Clear to land. Surface wind as met. report 030 08 knots
        QNH 1017
ACFT: 1017 clear to land, thank you

HEATHROW AIRPORT, LONDON

TWR: Tiger 10 hold at the top end of runway 23, I'll give you line up clearance shortly

ACFT: Tiger 10

TWR: Roger, 23. I've just seen a small amount of smoke come from — looks like the undercarriage. You check your temperatures

ACFT: Was that for Tiger 10?

TWR: Tiger 10 affirmative. Just saw a small amount of smoke come from — looks like the undercarriage. If you could check your brake temperatures

ACFT: OK, we're starting our inboard engines. I think it's probably coming from that

TWR: Roger, understood. Thanks Tiger 10

LONDON AIR TRAFFIC CONTROL CENTRE

ACFT: TA is now level at 60 and our main reason for diverting from Gatwick was an icing problem. We're now out of icing and we could continue to hold and go into Gatwick, if that's possible?

ACC: I'll keep you advised. In the meantime continue towards Midhurst TA

ACFT: Thank you sir. I'm sorry to be difficult but we are having problems as you are

ACC: Understood . . . TA I've just heard from Gatwick. In fact, they estimate because of the weight of the snow coming down, they're probably going to be snow clearing most of the morning anyway. So I think Hurn would be your best bet

ACFT: In that case would we make it Southampton?

ACC: That's no problem — Midhurst, Fawley for Southampton

ACFT: Thank you very much indeed sir

ACC: Dan-Air 401 and G- Correction Short 289 Gatwick expect snow clearance to be going on until at least mid-day today Dan-Air 401

ACFT: 401 understands Gatwick is going to be shut now until about mid-day for snow clearance.

Appendix 3

Listening Comprehensions and Answers to Exercises

Concordes

Unit 1

1.3 PHONETIC ALPHABET

Ex. 2

LIMA	19	74	ROMEO	113	PAPA	1004
MIKE	8	38	ECHO	343	INDIA	1015
FOXTROT	49	61	DELTA	595	JULIET	997
OSCAR	12	13	ALPHA	672	X-RAY	3000

Unit 2

2.2 READBACK

Ex. 1   Text

This is the text of what the controller (APP) says on tape. The words in italics show the correct readback of the instructions.

APP: Maintain *flight level 50*
Maintain *3000 feet QNH 1014*
Clear for straight in approach runway 23 QFE 1010, report final (*call you final*)
Clear to cross VFR
Turn *right heading 360* climb to *flight level 50*
Contact tower *118.4*

2.3 CORRECTION

Ex. 1   Text

1) ATSU: G-DO Caution. Marked trench right side, correction marked trench left side of entrance to apron

2) ATSU: Swissair 401 hold position. Aircraft on final for runway 28, correction runway 23

3) ATSU: Austrian 522 QNH 1015, correction QNH 1014

4) ATSU: Alitalia 293 contact London Control 129.5, correction 129.6

5) ATSU: Scandinavian 525 after the landing Boeing 727, correction Boeing 737 cross runway 28, correction 23. Report runway vacated

2.4 TRANSFER OF COMMUNICATION

Ex. 1   Text

TWR: Speedbird 350 contact London Control on 135.7
TWR: KD4150 Landing time 23 next turning right. Contact ground on 121.9
TWR: Air France 802 report leaving flight level 70. Contact Tower on 118.4
TWR: Iberia 210 contact Brussels Approach 119.2
TWR: Swissair 801 continue approach contact Munich Tower 119.7
TWR: Sabena 575 after departure continue straight ahead and contact Radar on 124.35

Answers

The frequencies heard are: 1) 135.7   3) 121.9   4) 118.4   7) 119.2
8) 119.7   10) 124.35

Unit 3

3.1 ATIS FOR DEPARTING FLIGHTS

Ex. 1   Text

Heathrow Departure information G, 08 45 hours weather 055° magnetic 08 knots temperature 9 dewpoint 3 QNH 1022 hectopascals. The departure runway now is 10 right

Answers

1) G GOLF   2) 08 45   3) a.m.   4) 9   5) speed 8 knots direction 055° magnetic   6) 1022 hPa   7) 10 right

Ex. 2   Text

Kastrup Departure information S,   19 30 hours weather 240° magnetic   10 knots temperature 16 dewpoint 7 QNH 1015 hPa. Runway in use 22 left

Answers

1) S   2) 19 30   3) 240°   4) 1015   5) 22 left

3.3 WEATHER INFORMATION

Ex. 1   **Text**

1) Marseilles FIR SIGMET timed 13 00 hours Marseilles FIR and southern Paris FIR, clear air turbulence reported flight level 200 to flight level 350 moderate to severe Marseilles SIGMET

2) Tunis VOLMET special broadcast 04 20 hours. Heavy sand-storm reported south of Tunis from ground level up to 10 000 feet Tunis-Carthage closed. Special SIGMET out

3) SIGMET Milan FIR timed at 00 01 hours Naples Airport closed due to earth tremors Milan FIR SIGMET out

4) F-LXOT windshear reported at 500 feet during last 30 minutes. F-OT cleared for take-off

Answers

1) a) 13 00, b) clear air turbulence, c) moderate *to* severe   2) a) south, b) 10 000, c) closed   3) a) Naples, b) earth tremors   4) 500

3.4 RVR REPORTING

Runway 26R	RVR touchdown 600 metres, midpoint 800 metres, stopend 700 metres
Runway 26L	RVR greater than 1100 metres
Runway 08R	RVR less than 100 metres

Ex. 1   **Answers**

1) touchdown 600, midpoint 800, stopend 700   2) greater than 1100 metres
3) less than 100 metres

Unit 4

4.1 PRE-FLIGHT RADIO CHECKS

Ex. 2

118.1, 120.4, 119.05, 122.75, 124.72, 124.47, 119.9, 119.1, 118.7, 121.1

4.2 ATC CLEARANCES

Ex. 1

1) ATSU: Clipper 281 cleared via flight planned route to Miami REKON 9 Departure, to cross REKON at 1400 hours flight level 50 squawk 3501

2) ATSU: Caledonian 511 cleared to London DARPA 27 Departure, to cross DARPA between 1405 and 1410

3) ATSU: N4081A is cleared to leave the zone north-east VFR QNH 1010

4.4 TAXI INSTRUCTIONS AND HOLDING INSTRUCTIONS BEFORE TAKE-OFF

1) ACFT: Ground Caledonian 211, stand C8 request taxi to holding point for runway 27

   GROUND: Caledonian 211 taxi to holding point X runway 27

2) ACFT: Ground Viasa 898, stand D2 request detailed taxi instructions for runway 27

   GROUND: Viasa 898 taxi via taxiways M and Z. Taxi with caution, marked trench right side of taxiway at holding point. Give way to Boeing 707 entering apron from taxiway

   ACFT: Traffic in sight Viasa 898

3) GROUND: Varig 451 hold short of taxiway N

   ACFT: Holding short Varig 451

4.5 PREPARATION FOR TAKE-OFF AND TAKE-OFF CLEARANCE

Ex. 1   Are you ready for departure?

1) Lot 771 are you ready for departure?

2) Line up and wait for landing Boeing 707 to vacate runway

3) Line up and take off runway 14

4) Be ready for immediate departure

5) Cleared for take-off runway 14. Take off immediately or vacate runway

6) Hold position, cancel take-off

7) Cleared for take-off wind 230° 7 knots

Unit 5

5.2 DEPARTING FLIGHTS TRANSFERRING FROM AERODROME RADAR TO AIRWAYS

Ex. 1 Listening comprehension

 Text

ACFT: Departure American 58 leaving 17 000* feet heading 050
DEP: American 58 radar contact. After 18 500** feet turn left heading 360
ACFT: After 18 500 feet turn left heading 360 American 58
DEP: American 58 turn left heading 320 to intercept the Mexico radial 343, direct to Monterrey
ACFT: Heading 320 to the 343 radial direct to Monterrey American 58
DEP: Correct

*one seven tousand
**one ait fife zero zero

Answers

1) Departure   2) American 58   3) 050   4) left   5) 343

Unit 6

6.4 LEVEL CHANGE INSTRUCTIONS

Ex. 1 Listening comprehension

 Text

1) ACC: Speedbird 439 descend to flight level 210 and report reaching
   ACFT: Speedbird 439 leaving flight level 290 for flight level 210

2) ACC: Kuwaiti 4447 climb to flight level 260 and call on reaching
   ACFT: Climb to flight level 260, leaving flight level 180 Kuwaiti 4447

3) ACC: Gulf 770 descend to flight level 170, report passing flight level 190
   ACFT: Roger Gulf 770 to flight level 170, report passing flight level 190

4) ACC: Air France 818 recleared to flight level 130 . . . Air France 818 descend to flight level 130
   ACFT: Descending to flight level 130 Air France 818

5) ACC: Saudi 770 descend to flight level 150 and report reaching
   ACFT: Descending to flight level 150 Saudi 770

Answers

1) flight level 290   2) flight level 180   3) flight level 190

4) descend. Aircraft did not respond to first call.   5) 150

6.5 TRAFFIC AND WEATHER INFORMATION AND AVOIDANCE

Ex. 1   1) ATSU: Saudi 909 Baghdad Control unknown traffic at 9 o'clock 5 miles crossing right to left

ACFT: Roger Saudi 909. Traffic not in sight. Request vectors

2) ATSU: Saudi 909 Baghdad Control avoiding action. Turn left immediately heading 330 unknown traffic closing at 12 o'clock

ACFT: Turning left heading 330 Saudi 909

3) ATSU: Saudi 909 Baghdad Control unknown traffic at 8 o'clock

ACFT: Looking out Saudi 909 (*later*) Traffic in sight Saudi 909

ATSU: Saudi 909 Baghdad Control now clear of traffic. Resume own navigation

ACFT: Roger Saudi 909

Unit 7

7.1 POSITION REPORTING

Ex. 1   1) Santa Monica Control N326AB over Santa Monica at 50 flight level 310 Gorman ETO 02 15

2) Santa Barbara Control N421LL over Gaviota at 01 13000 feet Santa Maria estimating at 55

3) Santa Barbara Control N122DE over Fillmore at 25 flight level 190 Santa Monica ETA 17 20

7.4 EN ROUTE HOLDING INSTRUCTIONS

Ex. 1   **Listening comprehension**

Text

1) ACC: American 326 Los Angeles Control

ACFT: Los Angeles Control American 326 go ahead

ACC: American 326 descend now to flight level 310 to be level by Foots. Hold at Foots flight level 310. Inbound track 322, right-hand pattern, report at Foots

2) ACC: Delta 435 Los Angeles Control
   ACFT: Los Angeles Control Delta 435 pass your message
   ACC: Delta 435 hold inbound on the 249 radial Los Angeles VOR between
           15 and 25 DME, right-hand pattern

Answers

1) descend   2) flight level 310   3) 322   4) 249   5) 15 and 25 DME

7.5 VOLMET METEOROLOGICAL BROADCASTS

This is Geneva Met. Broadcast met. report.

Geneva 1120. 040° 12 knots. Visibility 6 kilometres, mist. 2 octas 1500 feet, 8 octas 2500 feet, temperature 0, dewpoint −4, QNH 1019 nosig

Zurich 1120. 050° 10 knots. Visibility 6 kilometres, mist. 3 octas 1500 feet, 7 octas 1700 feet. Temperature −2, dewpoint −5 QNH 1021 nosig

Basle 1120. 100° 8 knots. Visibility 3500 metres, mist. 7 octas 2000 feet, temperature −0, dewpoint −4, QNH 1022 nosig

Ex. 1   Nicosia VOLMET broadcast

Text

Met. report:

06 40   Larnaca 340° 02 knots. Visibility 10 kilometres. 1 octa 3000 feet. Temperature 05, dewpoint 03, QNH 1023 nosig BREAK

06 50   Athinai calm, cavok. Temperature 06, dewpoint 02, QNH 1023 nosig BREAK

06 50   Rodhos calm, cavok. Temperature 09, dewpoint 04, QNH 1023 nosig BREAK

06 50   Ben Gurion 150° 06 knots, cavok. Temperature 09, dewpoint 04. QNH 1023 nosig BREAK

06 50   Ramat David missing BREAK

Answers

1) 06 40   2) no   3) calm (no wind)   4) 150° 06 knots   5) none

Ex. 2   VOLMET broadcast, second part

Text

06 00   Beirut 080° 06 knots. Visibility 10 kilometres, 2 octas 3000 feet. Temperature 07, dewpoint −00, QNH 1023 BREAK

06 00   Damascus 340° 01 knots, cavok. Temperature −03, dewpoint −04, QNH 1022 BREAK

06 00   Cairo 270° 04 knots. Visibility 7 kilometres in haze, 3 octas 2100 metres, temperature 08, dewpoint 02, QNH 1024 BREAK

06 20   Ankara calm. Visibility 2000 metres runway visibility 2200 metres. Fog patches, 3 octas 600 metres. Temperature missing, dewpoint missing, QNH 1022 BREAK

06 20   Istanbul 260° 14 knots, cavok. Temperature missing, dewpoint missing, QNH 1021 BREAK

Answers

1) 10 km,   2) −03,   3) 3 octas,   4) 1021

Unit 8

8.1 INITIAL CONTACT

Ex. 1   Listening comprehension

Text

ACFT: Tanga Approach 5Y-CDD
TWR: 5-DD Tanga Approach go ahead
ACFT: Tanga 5-DD Piper Arrow 25 miles east of your field. Heading 280 at 7000 feet VFR from Pemba to Tanga, estimating Tanga at 10 09, request joining instructions

ACFT: Pemba Tower 5Y-CCD
TWR: 5-CD Pemba Tower go ahead
ACFT: Pemba 5-CD Cessna 310 20 miles south-east of Mombasa. VFR from Malindi to Pemba, 6000 feet QNH 1021, estimating Pemba at 23 for landing

Answers

1) 25 miles   2) 280   3) 7000   4) 10 09   5) south-east   6) Malindi
7) 10 21   8) 23

Unit 9

9.1 ATIS FOR ARRIVING/DEPARTING FLIGHTS

Ex. 1   Text

Hong Kong International Airport information K. Runway-in-use 13. Expect IGS Approach. Surface wind 090 to 120° at 10 knots, visibility 10 kilometres, present weather haze. Cloud 1 octa at 3000 feet. Temperature 18, QNH 1023 mb. Acknowledge information K on frequencies 119.1 for arrivals, and 124.65 for departures.

ScaTTeRed = متفرقة سحب

BRoken = سحب متقطعة ترى السماء من خلالها

Ex. 2   Text

Warsaw information D. Landing runway 33, departure runway 29. Transition level 40. Wind variable 4 kilometres per hour. Visibility 10 kilometres, clouds 4 octas 800 metres, 5 octas 1500 metres. Temperature 9, dewpoint 5, QNH 1017 millibars, QFE 753 millimetres, 1004 millibars

Answers

1) Warsaw   2) D   3) departing   4) 40   5) variable 4 km/h   6) 10 km
7) 4   8) 1500 m   9) 5   10) QNH 1017 QFE 1004

9.2 INITIAL APPROACH CLEARANCE

Ex. 1   Listening comprehension

1) ACFT: Narita Arrival Korean 001 on 120.2 with R
   RADAR: Korean 001 Narita squawk 3444 ident
   ACFT: 3444 Korean 001
   RADAR: Korean 001 identified. Descend to 5000 feet QNH 1014. Heading 010. Radar vectors to a visual final runway 34. ILS unserviceable
   ACFT: (*readback*)

2) ACFT: Narita Arrival Singapore 505 heavy with X-ray
   RADAR: Singapore 505 Narita maintain flight level 100. Standard Martin Two arrival. After passing Martin descend to 9000 feet QNH 1020. Squawk 5610 ident. Number 5 in traffic. Report at Martin
   ACFT: (*readback*)

3) ACFT: Narita Arrival Speedbird 301 on 120.5 with D
   RADAR: Speedbird 301 Narita maintain flight level 100. Cleared to Mito for a Mito One arrival. After Mito descend to 8000 feet QNH 998. Number 6 in traffic RVR runway 16 1500 metres in drizzle. Squawk 5611 ident. Enter the hold at Lake and report
   ACFT: (*readback*)

Unit 11

11.3 RADAR VECTORING TO FINAL APPROACH

Ex. 1   Text

RADAR: G-DD 4 miles from touchdown height should be 1250 feet. Clear to land runway 21 surface wind 190° 10 knots. Right of track, turn left 5° heading 215. 3 miles from touchdown height should be 950 feet. On track turn right 5° heading 220. 2 miles from touchdown height should be 650 feet. Approach completed, out

ACFT: Runway in sight, G-DD

Answers

1) 1250 feet   2) right of centreline   3) 215   4) 2 miles

Unit 12

12.4 URGENCY MESSAGES AND ACKNOWLEDGEMENTS

Ex. 2   Completed dialogues

1) ACFT: PAN PAN PAN Le Touquet G-BCDO Cessna 150 departed Le Touquet 15 minutes ago. Having difficulty in cold front south of your airfield. Request QDMs back to Le Touquet urgently

TWR: Roger PAN G-BCDO. Transmit for direction

ACFT: G-BCDO one, two, three, two, one G-BCDO

2) ACFT: PAN PAN PAN Le Touquet Tower G-ABCO Piper Cherokee 3 p.o.b. Due severe turbulence request immediate diversion and joining instructions. 5 miles north of aerodrome at 2000 feet VFR heading 140 PPL with IMC.

TWR: G-ABCO Le Touquet Tower roger PAN. Descend to circuit height 1000 feet QFE 1008 and join base leg

12.5 EMERGENCY DESCENT

Ex. 2   **Completed dialogue**

ACFT (1):   MAYDAY   MAYDAY   MAYDAY   Lisbon   West,   Argentina   002
emergency descent

ACC: Argentina 002 squawk 7700 go ahead

ACFT (1):   Argentina 002 depressurised flight level 330. Descending rapidly
heading 180, approaching Narta reporting point

ACC: Argentina 002 roger MAYDAY, call when level. BREAK, BREAK.
Clipper 420 conflicting emergency traffic 12 o'clock 15 miles. Turn
left immediately heading 360 and descend to flight level 220

ACFT (2):   Clipper 420 turning left heading 360. Say again flight level

ACC: Descend to flight level 220 Lisbon West

ACFT (2):   Roger flight level 220 Clipper 420

Appendix 4

Keywords in Aviation English; Abbreviations

KEYWORDS

The number of the page where the word first appears is given in bold type beside each word.

Abeam   57
Advise (vb)   30
Airborne   20
Airway   16
Affirm   20
Altitude   5
Approach (vb)   19
Approved   16
Apron   17

Base   16
Box   37
Break   102

Calm   92
Cancel (vb)   47
Caution   22
Check (vb)   114
Circuit   17
Clearance   39
Cleared (vb)   16
Climb (vb)   21
Closing   66
Confirm (vb)   135
Contact (vb)   21
Continue (vb)   50
Cross (vb)   21

Departure   16
Descend (vb)   4
Dewpoint   26
Direct   52
Ditching   120
Divert (vb)   109
Downwind   16

Endurance   39
Established (vb)   100
Estimate (vb)   4
Expect (vb)   40
Expedite (vb)   44

Final   16
Fog   80

Give way (vb)   22
Glide path   100
Go ahead (vb)   4
Go around (vb)   108

Heading   1
Hectopascals   7
Height   5
Hold (vb)   20

Ice   30
Identification   111
Immediately   47
Information   15
Instructions   44

Join (vb)   16

Knots   26
Known traffic   55

Landing   91
Leave (vb)   15
Line-up (vb)   16
Localiser   100

Maintain (vb)   15
Magnetic   3
Mayday   120
Millibars   7
Minima   114
Missed approach   108
Monitor (vb)   23

Navigation   67
Negative   20

Observe (vb)   79
Octa   80
Orbit   76
Outer marker   100
Overhead   84

Pan   128
Pass (vb)   25
Position   13
Push-back (vb)   16

Radar   24
Range   101
Reach (vb)   59
Readability   37
Readback (vb)   20
Report (vb)   13
Request (vb)   16
Resume (vb)   67
Roger   4
Runway   1

Slot-time   40

Snow   30
Squawk   39
Stand-by   40
Start-up (vb)   17

Take-off (vb)   47
Taxi (vb)   44
Taxiway   22
Temperature   26

Terminate (vb)   114
Threshold   30
Touchdown   20
Track   76
Traffic   55
Trench   22
Turn (vb)   21

Undercarriage   132

Unknown   66
Unserviceable   30

Vacate (vb)   22
Visibility   35
Visual   89

Wilco   59
Windshear   33

ABBREVIATIONS

The number of the page where the abbreviation is first used (and explained) is given in bold type beside each abbreviation.

ACC   50
ACFT   5
APP   5
ATCO   11
ATIS   15
ATSU   4

CB   33
CTZ   19

DF   129
DME   40

EAT   109
ETA   13
ETO   69

FIR   33

FIS   55

hPa   26

IFR   39
IGS   94
ILS   101
IMC   55

mb   26

NDB   99

OCA   114
OCH   114

QDM   129

QFE   7
QNH   7

RVR   34

SID   39
SIGMET   33
SRA   114
STAR   96

TMA   19
TWR   5

VFR   39
VMC   55
VOLMET   33
VOR   76

Z (zulu)   55

A History of
Moseley
Village

Norman Hewston

Foreword by Carl Chinn

GU00580212

AMBERLEY

Dedicated to all Moseley villagers, past, present and future.
Please look after her.

First published 2009

Amberley Publishing Plc
Cirencester Road, Chalford,
Stroud, Gloucestershire, GL6 8PE

www.amberley-books.com

British Library Cataloguing in Publication Data.
A catalogue record for this book is available from the British Library.

ISBN 978 1 84868 141 5

Typesetting and Origination by FONTHILLDESIGN.
Printed in the UK.

Contents

Foreword

Most of my life I have lived in and around Moseley. Mom and Dad moved from rooms in Newton Road, Sparkhill to 26, Westlands Road just before I was born in 1956. We grew up in what was like a little village made up of Westlands, Eastlands, Southlands and Northlands Roads, along with part of Billesley Lane. Our friends lived round the corner, people like Jane Albutt, Brian Jobson, Gareth Nicholas, Trevor Smith and others, and we'd play out safely on the streets till late in the light nights. We had a poisonous brook, or so we thought, that stopped us from getting into the unknown world of Moseley Golf Club from the bottom of Northlands, and we even had our own nurse. Nurse Legge was a retired woman to whom you could always run for help and advice. To us as children, most of the neighbours were known as Mr or Mrs, and then their surname, but we were very close to Jane's mom and she was always Aunt Nancy to us. She was a very special neighbour and a very special family friend.

The village feel locally was enhanced by our own shops. My first errand on my own was to Blenheim Stores, now Mill's Stores, just across Billesley Lane. That's where Mom bought some of her groceries, although she also shopped a lot down the lane, the Ladypool Road where Dad came from. There was a sweet shop alongside the stores which had a Lucky Dip. Here we could spend coppers on black jacks and fruit salads, flying saucers and kayli. On the opposite corner, across Blenheim Road itself, was Sims the greengrocer's. When I was a toddler I loved strawberries so much that they had to cover them up when they saw Mom approaching the shop with me and Our Darryl, or else I'd be picking up all the punnets for Mom to buy.

We even had our own butcher at the end of our road, Mr Nickless, whose shop proclaimed 'Home Killed Meat' and a few yards away on the corner of Southlands Road was an 'outdoor' (off-licence). Just a bit further along Billesley Lane was Greenhill Garage, which is still providing a fine service; and then came a little sweet shop on the corner of Greenhill Road.

If we needed something other than these shops could provide, Mom would send us up Cambridge Road to the Co-op in King's Heath Village, where we would also go for Saturday matinees at the 'Kingsway' to see films featuring the likes of Morecambe and Wise, and Norman Wisdom.

Our world stretched out when we started school at Moseley Church of England. This was at the old buildings, since knocked down, in School Road. It was a strange experience as my great grandfather, Richard Chinn, had gone there in the 1870s when it had been set amongst fields. As we got older, a teacher would sometimes send us into Moseley Village to fetch something for them. It's not something you would do today. Shops I recall well are Simpson's the fishmonger, Gascoigne's the funeral director's, Drucker's with their cakes, and the Stoneleigh Dog Shop. Of course, however, the dominant building in the village was St Mary's Church, where we had ancestors buried in the churchyard and to which we would go from school at Easter and Christmas especially.

When I was ten, Mom and Dad moved near to the Ford at the River Cole by Sarehole Mill. Technically the new address still came under Moseley, but we now felt closer to the adjoining districts of Springfield, Sparkhill and Hall Green. Still, Moseley continued to be important in our lives as Darryl and I both went on to attend Moseley Grammar and supported Moseley Rugby Club. I still live close to Moseley and I am delighted to have had the opportunity to learn more about this vibrant and distinctive district in Norman Hewston's deeply researched book. This is a monumental work that is a tribute to Norman's determination and vigour as a researcher. It brings together in an exciting way both text and photographs and in so doing highlights the history of a thriving modern suburb. I congratulate Norman on his achievement.

Carl Chinn MBE

Introduction

It is no easy task to write a history of a district, which has, for the most part, remained open fields and pasture until relatively recent times. Even harder is it to construct such a narrative from the often sketchy details that have survived in the public records — scant details of landowners and the faded memories of local people of bygone time — and still make the story interesting.

Whether or not I have succeeded in this endeavor is, of course, for the reader to decide. But, fortunately, the Victorian village with ancient roots has, as always, some very interesting and colorful characters to illustrate its history.

Having been a member of Moseley community for the best part of a decade, since a quarter of a century ago, like so many who have moved away, I have never forgotten the spirit, particularly at that time, of its diverse population and what the locals often referred to as the 'Magic of Moseley'.

This was nothing you could put your finger on — that is, it was not tangible — and was something that could only be experienced by living in Moseley, not just as a visitor passing through.

In the years since my departure, images of the old village have continued to fascinate me, and as I sought after them I gradually built up a large collection of photographs and postcards of the area along with other related documentation and ephemera, much of which illustrates this book.

On setting out to gather information for this project, however, the first thing I became aware of was just how little has actually been written about Moseley compared to that of its neighboring areas. A valuable source of reference has been Alison Fairn's *A History of Moseley* — this being the only other book on the subject that I am aware of. Readers familiar with that work will no doubt recognise that I have consulted many of the original sources of information that she utilised, but also there is much which was unavailable to her at the time of her writing in the early 1970s.

In her concluding chapter, 'Moseley 1945-1970', Miss Fairn wrote that it was too early to write up a history of Moseley in the 1970s, 'but there was confidence that some future historian would find it deeply interesting'. It is my hope that this work will prove to be a worthy companion to hers. Another valuable source has been the *Moseley Society Journal,* published under several similar titles between 1891 and 1933. This was so fascinating and informative that I have given the publication its own chapter within this book.

The Moseley Trail, printed in 1986 by Birmingham Urban Studies Centers Committee, took the form, as the title suggests, of a trek on foot through the village, describing the history and architecture of the area along the way. This is a very good and effective method, which I have employed in two chapters of this book, under the titles 'The General Development of Moseley' and 'The Development of the High Street'.

I would like to make mention of two other books, which perhaps complete the short list of published sources on Moseley village. They are *Moseley, Balsall Heath and Highgate*, compiled by Marian Baxter and Peter Drake, and, number 6 in the series, *Yesterday's Warwickshire*, which dealt with Moseley and King's Heath and was written by John Marks, although these last two publications consist chiefly of photographs and postcards, with the relevant information being conveyed in captions.

Aside from providing the reader with a fascinating history of 'the village', as it is still affectionately known by locals, I have attempted to describe and illustrate what has been sadly lost to the passing of time. This has been done in the hope that it will make more people aware of, amongst other things, the rich architectural heritage (with its twenty-six listed buildings) that is Moseley and, therefore, hopefully go some way towards preventing the destruction of yet more of its earlier and irreplaceable establishments, which help retain the village's links with its prosperous and much-lamented past.

In order to chart these changes, I have used numerous old photographic references, many from the Victorian and Edwardian era. In this modern age of heavy traffic, I have also taken my life in my hands to stand as closely as possible (often in the middle of the road) to the same position as the photographers of those earlier times when taking the original pictures, so that accurate comparisons can be made between now and then.

In these scenes, the reader will not fail to note the absence of traffic, congestion and litter; perhaps the only unsightly clutter being the tramlines and cables, and the only reference to pollution being the horse droppings in the otherwise deserted roadways.

Traffic aside I had, on occasion, to run the gauntlet of suspicious residents when taking some of these shots.

'Why are you doing taking pictures of my house?'

'I'm NOT taking pictures of your house madam — I'm taking pictures of the street.'

'Why?'

I have also met many kind, helpful and supportive people along the way, and I would like to convey my gratitude to them for their time, advice, loan of materials and encouragement during the time I have been engaged in this project. I, of course, make no claims as to infallibility concerning this material, although I have done my best to verify from the available sources, sometimes conflicting information. It is inevitable, however, that the occasional error here and there may have crept in, particularly where corroborating documentation is a little thin on the ground. Never the less, it is my hope that I have been able to present the reader with a reliable and worthy account of Moseley Village through time.

Acknowledgements

During the course of compiling this book I have received help and encouragement from so many people, and whilst it would be impossible to name all of them, I would particularly like to thank the following:

For use of photographs and postcards: Andrew Maxam, Barrie Geens, Jean Eustace, Joyce Elliott, Hilary Mc Geown, Janet Naylor, Bill Hulse and Brett Wilde. Brett is the official photographer for the *Birmingham 13* magazine and many of his very imaginative pictures are contained in this work.

Many thanks also to Fiona Adams of The Moseley Society. Fiona opened up her photographic archives and afforded me access to much of her *Birmingham 13* magazine collection, as well as helping out with all sorts of other queries along the way. My gratitude goes also to The Moseley Local History Society for their various publications to which I have referred, and Roy Cockel, of that body, who was of great assistance to me in obtaining images from the collection.

Professor Carl Chinn MBE gave me much advice and assistance through his Birmingham Life Collection and *Brummagem* magazine, for which I am grateful. The (almost) ever-available staff of Birmingham Public Library likewise made accessible so much material from their collection that was relevant to this book, and I am not going to forget Kerry Fair of King's Heath Library because she dug out no small amount of documentation about Moseley Village and even put it all aside for me to go through.

There are, of course, many others who have furnished me with anecdotes and recollections of the village in times gone by and, though nameless, I would like to thank all these also.

Many of the images in this work are public domain, given their age, and where possible I have cited details of source or original ownership but, of course, there are also many whose origins I have been unable to trace.

Last, but not least, I must thank my lovely wife Diane for all the help she has given to me in putting this book together and for driving me to and around the village whenever necessary for me to get photographs and collect information.

ONE

The Seventeenth Century

Establishment: the First Village to the Seventeenth Century

In what exact period of time the first settlers arrived in the area, which we now know as Moseley, just outside Birmingham, is difficult to say. Of equal uncertainty is who exactly they were. What we do know is that there were dwellers in the vicinity at least 3,000 years ago. This was established by the discovery in 1980 of two Bronze Age burnt mounds in Moseley Bog, the charcoal from which gave archaeologists a radiocarbon date of around 1100 BC. The mounds, of which there were two, consisted of a layer of heat-shattered stones, the purpose of which is also open to conjecture, one theory being that the stones were heated in fires to produce hot water for cooking. However, the absence of remains related to this activity, particularly of bones, has cast doubt on this and some have suggested that the hot water produced was for bathing, dyeing or the treatment of leather. An alternative theory is that the mounds were debris from some type of primitive sauna, as has been used by Native American Indians in times past, by erecting a tent or hut over a pool of heated stones. Whatever the reason, the existence of these mounds and similar, found on Moseley Golf Course and in Highbury Park, suggest that there was human activity in this location around the Bronze Age.

During the following epoch, the Iron Age, the area which we today call Birmingham was the borderland of three different tribes of Celtic people. To the east of Birmingham were the Corieltauvi, whose capital was Leicester. To the west with Wrekin as their capital, were the Cornovil, and to the south, in the area of interest to us, the Dobunii, who had their capital in Cirencester.

An earthworks, which existed in Victorian times until ploughed away, at the location of what is now the playing field of Windermere Road near Swanshurst Park, has led to speculation that it was used by King Alfred during his war with the Danes, but this is very unlikely. Furthermore, by its description, it might well have been of prehistoric date.

Of the Roman period of British occupation, there are no known remains in the area of Moseley, although there have been, from time to time, reports of Roman coins found about the district. The Romans had kilns in Alcester, and although it has been suggested that they may have come to Moseley for a supply of rich clay, there is as yet no proof that this was the case.

Moseley first makes its appearance on record as 'Museleie'. This is the first recorded reference to the place and it comes to us through the Domesday Book of 1086, in which it is included as one of the eighteen *Berewicks*, or colonies of *Bremesgroev* (Bromsgrove). There may have been a settlement on this site for some centuries before, but as far as we can tell, Celts aside, the first Moseleians were perhaps the descendants of the West Saxons, whose fore-fathers were known as *Hwicce*, * who are believed to have replaced the *Dobunii*. *Hwicca: **Wychwood, Whichford, Whichenford, Wych** and **Whycbury** all derive from the name of this Saxon tribe.

The *Hwicce* settled in South Worcestershire at the end of the sixth century AD, establishing themselves in *Bremesgrefan*. They later had their tribal capital as *Wirecestre* (Worcester). From Bromsgrove during the following century, their descendants travelled along the old crumbling Roman highway (Bristol Road) to occupy Norton (North Farm, later King's Norton) and 'Moseley', as well as other locations on the Lickey slopes. They probably followed the ridge on the east side of the river Rea, along an existing track, in search of grazing pastures for their livestock, until they came to a level bench of dry soil, and here, amidst a woodland clearing, they erected wooden huts and shelters, henceforth establishing a new community.

To the south and east lay stony heath-land, whilst west and north of the ridge oak forests rose upon the valley flanks. Boggy meadows straddled the edges of the winding river, which could be dammed to provide food and water.

The Saxon village was probably no more than a small grouping of mud and timber-frame thatched shelters, erected within a circle and surrounded by a tall fence, in-turn enclosed within a defensive ditch as protection against wolves, bears and even marauding strangers. Herd and livestock too would be brought within the enclosure at night for safekeeping.

Where exactly the first village was situated is also unknown. One theory is that it was located along the Alcester Road, between St Mary's church and what, since 1900, has been known as The Parade. Another plausible theory places it near the junction of Church and Wake Green Roads, and uphill from the current-day village centre.

Here, it can be observed, the road from St Mary's Row, just beyond the church lynch gate, swings to the left towards Church Road before arching back onto Wake Green Road. This suggests that the original route, instead of running straight, had to bypass or skirt some obstruction that lay in its path. As the route is an ancient one that followed a track linking the Rivers Rea and Cole, this diversion was likely established in Saxon times.

Could this be the original settlement site, as has been suggested? This location is indeed a dry bench of land close to an ideal water source. Here also, another ancient track crossed the Rea and Cole as a southern route into Birmingham, from what are now School and Church Roads. These tracks were probably in regular use until the sixteenth century. Thereafter, another was eventually cut across heath-land to the Alcester Road, so that the earlier track would have fallen into disuse through neglect.

If the original settlement *was* east of St Mary's church, it could perhaps explain the reason why an Elizabethan timber-framed farmstead, which apparently once stood on

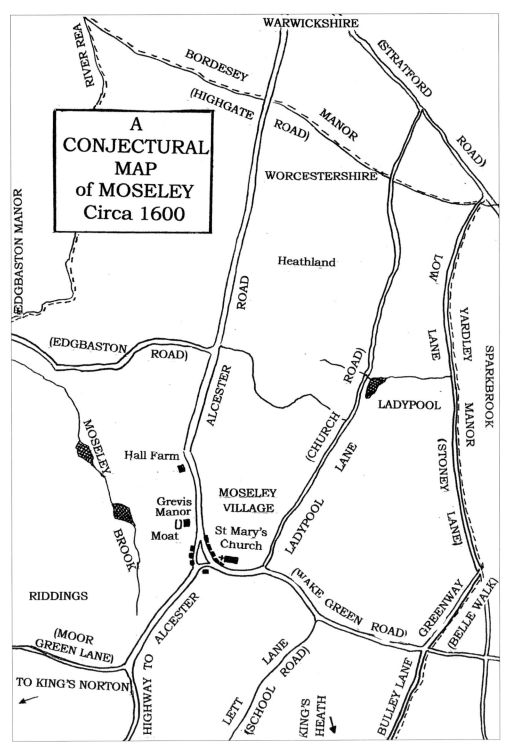

WARWICKSHIRE

RIVER REA

BORDESEY

(STRATFORD ROAD)

(HIGHGATE ROAD)

MANOR

WORCESTERSHIRE

A
CONJECTURAL
MAP
of MOSELEY
Circa 1600

EDGBASTON MANOR

Heathland

LOW LANE

YARDLEY MANOR

SPARKBROOK

(EDGBASTON ROAD)

ALCESTER ROAD

(CHURCH ROAD)

LADYPOOL

MOSELEY

Hall Farm

Grevis Manor

Moat

MOSELEY VILLAGE

St Mary's Church

LADYPOOL LANE

(STONEY LANE)

BROOK

RIDDINGS

(MOOR GREEN LANE)

TO KING'S NORTON

HIGHWAY TO ALCESTER

LETT LANE

(SCHOOL ROAD)

KING'S HEATH

(WAKE GREEN ROAD)

GREENWAY

BULLEY LANE

(BELLE WALK)

Map *c.* 1600.

the site, was known as the Village Green House. This was demolished to make way for a large Georgian building known as Elmshurst, which eventually suffered the same fate. The name of the Elizabethan house may well have recalled a time when the green was further up the hill; meaning that the village relocated to its present position at some later period of time.

Doubt too is cast on the origin and meaning of the village name and there are at least two theories. As mentioned, the first recorded name of the village comes from the Domesday Book, where it is rendered 'Museleie' thought to be from the Old English *Mus (a)-leage* or 'field mice clearing'.

The second derivation interprets 'Mose' as 'Moss' (alluding to the boggy ground around the village), and hence 'bog clearing'. Indeed, there is another 'Moseley' in Worcestershire, to which this rendition applies. However, the 'Moseley' that is the subject of this work is not referred to as 'Moselege' until 1221. *The Oxford Names Companion*, whilst acknowledging that the obvious derivation from the Old English would be Mos (relating to peat bog and leah-wood, clearing) states that the 'Moseley' south of Birmingham and referred to in the Domesday Book as 'Museleie' had as the first element the Old English *Mus*, meaning 'mouse', whilst another 'Moseley' in Staffordshire, referred to in the Domesday Book as 'Molesleie', had the genitive case of the Old English byname *Moll*. The original use of the words 'mouse clearing' may also

This lovely old medieval timber-framed house stood for centuries on Edgbaston Lane until it was demolished in the 1890s when road widening took place.

have denoted a small glade. Interestingly, one of the smallest fields in Yardley, right up to 1847, was known as Mouse Park. Either way, the earliest reference in the Domesday Book records William the Conqueror as holding 'Bremesgrove' in demesne with its eighteen berewicks, including 'Museleie' and 'Nortune' being in the *Came Hundred*, which is the Anglo-Saxon unit for administration and justice, usually comprising of 100 families. It was a fair jaunt for family heads to travel to Came Moot, which was at Lickey, in order to observe secular and spiritual affairs!

On the other side of the Rea there dwelt another group of settlers who were also of Germanic origin: the Anglian folk. They had come to occupy the Midlands from the north-east and in so doing established settlements in Aston, Birmingham, and Edgbaston amongst other places. The establishment of parishes in the area came about in 680 AD when Worcester became the seat of a bishop. Bromsgrove thus became the centre of a large parish, including King's Norton, of which Moseley was its northernmost part. From the thirteenth century, Nortune became a separate manor, which covered twelve thousand acres. However, it remained a dependant chapelry of Bromsgrove until 1846. Kings Norton itself was a royal possession until purchased from the crown (along with Moseley) by John Taylor in 1804.

By 1176, Moseley was described as being in the Hundred of Halfshire and as property of the crown it was given over for use of the favourites of the monarchy, but in the thirteenth century it came into possession of the Mortimer family. According to the eighteenth-century historian Nash, it again reverted to the crown through the marriage of Edward Mortimer and Phillipa, granddaughter of Edward III and ancestress of Edward IV. The manor was often the possession of queen consorts, as was the case in 1494 when Henry VII's wife, Queen Elizabeth, granted land at Moseley for the building of a chapel. Jane Seymour, the third wife of Henry VIII, is named in connection with a local land-related case and later, in 1629, so is Henrietta Maria, wife of Charles I, who angered landowners by trying to enclose wasteland.

Surviving land-transaction records document some of the earlier local people, and equally interesting are the names of fields, meadows and pasture involved in the transactions.

John Farmon, who lived in King's Norton in 1327, is thought to have had land in Moseley named after him. A 'grant from Robert Jordan to Richard de la Grene of Moselee of land in Moselee' dates from the thirteenth century, whilst another, obviously relating to the same family and dated 14 October 1319, records a similar contract between 'Richard son of John Atte Grene, of Moseleye and Geoffrey le Berch and Edith, his wife, of land at Kyngeshet.' Likewise, a 'Release of Richard Atte Grene of Moseleye to Geoffre le Schepehurde of Moseleye and Edith, his wife of land in Moseleye dated at Moseleye Friday next after the feast of St Michael 16th December 1335.'

Another grant from John de Walstode, a merchant, to John Costenoth, rector of the church of Darlaston, John Piddoke, chaplain of Birmingham, Thomas O' the Heth of Walsale (Walsall) and Richard 'son of the said John de Walstode, of land called Wallemesdowe in Moseley. Dated at Kingesnorton, in the feast of St Matthew the Apostle and Evangelizer 21st September 1391.'

There are further grants from 'Richard Brown of Moseley to Thomas O' the Feld son of William O' the Feld, of land in a field called Brodefield in Moseley', which is dated 2 February 1443, and 'John Sergeannt, alias John Sannson, of Kyngesnorton to John son of Thomas Greve, of Kyngesnorton, of land in Moseley called 'Le Lye', which is dated 12 January 1438/9.

A release from Sarah Bedull to her son names a croft of land called Smithslond in Moseley and dates from the Feast of the Nativity, 25 December 1436.

The Guild of Moseley is mentioned in a counterpart indenture between William Bromege, late of Moseley, John Raynolde, John Slought and Henry Slought. This is dated November 1465.

During the reign of Henry VIII, Moseley was a member of the Guild of Knowle, when, it is recorded, 134 inhabitants of King's Norton and Moseley had their names entered upon the register thereof. One of these was Thomas Grevis, who in 1520 was a Master of the Guild, a position 'seldom attained by any but substantial men'. He, having been elected to preside at the annual meeting of the Guild, made a big impression after bringing with him as many friends, neighbours, tenants and members of both religious and secular society as he could muster. There were many benefits to belonging to the Guild, not least of which was temporal relief during times of sickness or distress, as well as masses for the 'repose of the soul after death'.

Moseley Juxta receives a mention among the inquisitions in the Tower of London, having 6 messuages in 10 acres of land in 1481/2.

In 1490, Maurice Weeld and Robert Bayle, both tithing men, contested the actions of William Hawkes, who it seems dispensed with planning permission and commenced to 'build a house upon the common at Moseley to the injury of the tenants without license from the Lady of the Manor'. In this petition there is also mentioned ground near 'Hethland' (obviously 'heath land').

[A] deed poll whereby Humfrey More of Moseley grants to John Rawelyns of Malverne Magna Great Malvern, County of Worcestershire, yeoman, John Moer, the elder, Roger Biddill and Arthur Parkes of Moseley, nayler, a tenement and land called Le Ruddynges and other lands in Moseley [this is dated 14 November 1555]

Star Chamber Proceedings during the reign of King Henry VIII, between plaintiff Roger Grafton and the Town Clerk of Worcester, William Lyttelton as defendant, accuses him of 'Forgery of deeds relating to rental of a tenement at Moseley.'

Going through these records, it is clear that in some cases the land being transacted has been named after its owner, as perhaps is the case with reference to Smitheslond in 1436: possibly the same land recorded later in 1456 as Smytheslong. This may also be the case with Wallemdowe in 1319, as a later reference of 1464 gives us the name Wallenlandes. Others from fifteenth and sixteenth-century documents include Richardsmedow, Wardesmedow and Wyllyotts. It is also apparent that some of these names are of early English and Norman origin, whilst others appear to be derived from topographic descriptions. Typical of this is a later reference relating to the Warwickshire family of Greswald, dated 1635/6, which alludes to '... property near Camphill in Bordesley and thereabout... Long Acres in Moseley... amongst other lands and a croft of four acres in Moseley.'

The names of other fields and lots of land that have come down to us remain a mystery, like Shytterokk (Shutlock?), Cokrlyflis and Hemeryes (Henburys?). The tithe map of 1840 preserves many early names, which, no doubt, once more derive their names from one-time owners, such as Wavings Lower Dunwells, Leasow and Vaughtons Meadow.

Many other obviously very early names also survived to be recorded on the same tithe map, including Mill Phlegm, Shuttrick Mead and Shoulder of Mutton Piece. References to Hundreds Meadow and Big Hundreds Meadow may hint to us of the locations of the Saxon hundred court, where legal administration of the settlement was carried out.

During the Middle Ages, the village is believed to have consisted of somewhere between ten and twenty low half-timbered houses clustered around an acre of roughly-triangular green. One of these was an open-fronted blacksmith's forge, which stood alongside an alehouse, the forerunner of the later Bull's Head.

At this time, there were no crossroads and the present building lines of Alcester Road and St Mary's Row may indicate for us the original size of the 'village green' before road widening helped to shrink it to the size we see it today.

To the west, the sunken highway meandered onto Norton and Birmingham, and to the east of the green a rough rutted-track was carved up the hill to St Mary's and onwards, forking into separate tracks leading north to Ladypool and eastward to the Grevis' Lady Mill on Coldbath Brook and Swanshurst.

The first corn mills were established by the lords of the manor, who in turn charged for the use thereof. In the sixteenth century, there was a blade mill known as Moor Green Forge and another, Wake Green Mill, is recorded in a deed dated 1664 as being the property of Richard Grevis, this being in the vicinity of what we now know as Moseley Bog.

Another document of the same year gives mention to Sir Richard Grevis also coming into the possession of 'Wake Green Militia'.

The Grevis clan — pronounced Greeves/Greve and spelt variously — were a yeoman family who had profited much from the procurement of cheap land confiscated from the church during the Dissolution under Henry VIII (1536). Later, the family occupied Moseley Hall, which at this time may have stood where King Edward Road is now. Moseley had been known as a manor from around 1456, and some time towards the end of the fifteenth century, it is thought that they erected their new hall (originally a moated manor) on the opposite side of the road, sitting back from the highway. This was perhaps towards the north end of the village, roughly somewhere behind the present Presbyterian church on Chantry Road corner.

The only description we have of Moseley Hall, which, most unfortunately, was torn down in 1842, comes from two rough drawings made in 1802 and 1830. These show the property to have been a medieval-style hall, built, apparently, brick-free and in herringbone timber style, with gabled wings of a later period on either flank. It was tiled and had three stone chimney-clusters, with out buildings separating it from the highway. To the rear of the hall lay Moseley Brook (now Moseley Private Park), where fishponds had been formed. Opposite, during the eighteenth century, stood The Old Swan Inn and behind this open field all the way to Ladypool Lane (now Church Road).

It is likely that there was a connection between Moseley and the Cistercians of Bordesley Abbey near Redditch, which was founded by the Empress Matilda in 1138. The order is thought by some local historians to have established a chantry chapel in Moseley; this may have stood on the present site of St Mary's or, alternatively, in or close by what we now know as Chantry Road. This would have been a private chapel, which required the mandate from the Pope granting permission for the local parishioners to use it as a place of worship. That the Cistercian Order did indeed possess land in the manor of King's Norton during the thirteenth century seems certain, and a court case dating to 1514 records a dispute over tithes between the Prior of Worcester and the Abbot of Bordesley. Further, a grange in King's Norton is recorded amongst the possessions of Bordesley Abbey at the Dissolution, but other than this reference, there seems to be no other documentation to prove the existence of a chapel in Moseley before the sixteenth century.

There were as yet no schools in Moseley, unless some form of tuition on the part of the parish priests existed. It is likely that the sons of local gentry would have to take a horse and ride over to the Free Grammar School, which had opened in King's Norton in 1536 but which was closed four years later when property of the church was being seized by the crown during the Dissolution. It was, however, allowed to re-open during the brief reign of Edward VI.

Being one of five tax yields in King's Norton, Moseley was entitled to a 'thirdborough', or village constable, as well as its own 'ale-taster'. These, like others, engaged in the basic administration of affairs in the village, received no wages but were entitled to expenses. These 'offices' were, until Tudor times, the domain of the tenant-in-chief or his steward and thereafter it fell to the local squire and JP.

With the decline of the manorial courts system, the parish took over the role of local government by levying rates, caring for the poor and maintaining the highway, but chief tenants also played their part by holding office in turn.

The Black Death must have depleted the already small population of the village and no doubt caused problems for the lord of the manor, being unable to find workers to cultivate the demesne lands. Added to this, many tenants preferred to pay in coin for their rent instead of working for it. Some of these tenants took to acquiring vacant holdings and grouping their lands, which were often given over to pasture, replacing arable farming. After all, it took few men to look after sheep and the wool trade was flourishing (King's Norton had done very well from it). As a result of these problems, some lords had their tenants evicted from the land, pulled down or raised their dwellings to the ground and had the land enclosed. Although there is no evidence that this actually happened in Moseley, it certainly did elsewhere. Land in Moseley was to remain open for at least a few centuries longer.

During the political instability of the seventeenth century, the ordinary village folk no doubt tried to get on with their lives and may have shown little allegiance to either King or Parliament, although they were at times heavily taxed and it doubtless fell upon them to provide billet, board and fare for the forces of both sides.

There is, however, at least one story that seems to have survived from the period of the civil war, which, when printed in the *Moseley Society Journal* in 1895, under the title 'A Moseley Romance of Two Centuries Ago', was said to have been reconstructed from a diary. A few faded letters, which were at that time in the possession of an unnamed lady in Edgbaston, related to a local royalist, one Sir Roger Seaton, and his good lady wife, Doris Seaton, who lived, as far as it could be ascertained, a short way off the Moseley

The splendid alabaster tomb of Sir Richard Grevis, who died in 1632, and his wife Anne
Leighton, in St Nicholas' church, King's Norton. The Grevis family owned extensive lands both
in and around the village and lived at the original Moseley Hall, which stood on the site of the
Parade on the High Street.

Road. The period of time, although only days and months were given, was evidently shortly after the establishment of the Commonwealth (1649), following the execution of Charles I and when anyone with Royalist sympathies, especially if they had taken up arms against Parliament, had to escape, or at least keep a low profile.

Sir Roger Seaton had, according to the writings, '... suffered sorely in the skirmish by Prince Rupert round and about Berminghame'. Enduring much pain, loss of blood and lack of adequate treatment for his wounds, and 'longe hiding from the ennemie', the knight eventually made it back to his home, where, it was hoped, he could remain hidden in a concealed and narrow room at his house, until his wounds were healed and he was strong enough to be able to flee to France, as many Royalists were obliged to do. With Cromwell's men ever on the lookout for Royalists and Royalist sympathisers, Sir Roger's whereabouts were kept secret, being known only to his wife and one faithful servant, who communicated with him via a covert door-mechanism that was unobvious to others. For many months he remained here, tended faithfully by his wife, who dressed and cleaned his wounds regularly and prayed for his recovery. At length they suddenly received news from one of their children, who had been playing in the long lane leading to the house, that 'rough men', who were treading down the flowers, were on their way to the house saying they would 'have the blood of a traitor'.

As Lady Doris yet heard this report, she could see the soldiers coming into sight. Without a moment to lose she hurried to her husband and informed him of what was happening. She helped him prepare to flee, with their faithful servant, through a window from his concealed quarters, but this, she instructed the servant, they must do both hastily and quietly whilst she went down to divert the soldiers. Leaving the embrace of her husband, she returned to the hall where she received the unwanted guests without an apparent care in the world, even smiling happily and responding to their demands, saying:

> Search by all means. Far be it from me to hinder you who are as I am, loyal servants of our good Protector, but before you begin your work, about which I am sure there has been some misruling, for you see me and all my household round me and no traitor hidden for you to seek, let me beg you to drink.

Eagerly taking up the offer, the soldiers seated themselves and were so served. Lady Doris then suggested she entertain them further by performing a dance that she had learnt 'in the old evil days before good Puritan rule fell upon this land' and which now, by Puritan law, was strictly forbidden.

Lifting her skirts, Lady Doris revealed more leg than a man was want generally to see in those times, especially those of a respectable woman, and she danced for them a jig, which had in earlier days endeared her to Queen Henrietta Maria herself at Royal Court. Flushed of face and wide eyed, with the secret door behind her, she 'danced the dance on which a life dearer than hers depended'. Listening hard above the patter of her dainty feet, she heard the opening of the window, followed by the short laboured breaths of her dear husband, and the creak of hemp as the ropes lowered him to the ground, and as she did, she danced more urgently, keeping the attention of the supping soldiery seated before. On she danced, almost breathlessly, anticipating the sudden clatter of horses hooves on the cobbled ground as they bore her husband away... but, this she did not hear, so continued to dance for all he was to her worth, not daring one moment to cease the entertainment of her entranced audience. But then, she caught sight of her trusted servant standing in the doorway, 'his face white as ashes' and beckoning her to follow. The dancing ceased and she followed him out to the courtyard where the body of her husband lay. The strain had been too much and he expired just as he had reached the ground and before he could be raised to the saddle. Death had come at last, quickly and painlessly.

The edited story was concluded by saying that these details were all that it was possible to assemble from the almost undecipherable writing which had been handed down, but went on to say:

> Only two things may be told. Cromwell's soldiers never let their master know that they were baulked of their prey by a dancing Delilah, and there is an old house in Moseley standing to this day where every now and then may be heard the patter of a woman's feet, when no woman can be seen, dancing as madly and stopping as suddenly as did the Lady Doris more than 200 years ago.

TWO

The Eighteenth Century
The Beginning of Development

During the early 1700s, Moseley was still a small hamlet straddling rutted tracks between Birmingham and King's Norton. Travellers took to these routes at their peril, for they were treacherous in places, and as a result the village still remained, for the most part, self-sufficient. The hazards of travel remained until the new Turnpike Road to Alcester was built later in the century.

At this time, the village consisted of a few timber-framed houses stretching from the present-day Fighting Cocks, round St Mary's Row and up to the chapel. There were also a few such houses the other side of Alcester Road, with the old Grevis Hall a few yards on. Further up, towards present-day Park Hill, was Hall Farm. There were other outlaying farms as well; amongst these were Swanshurst (dating to 1662), Moorcroft and Fleetwoods, near what was later to become Anderton Park Road. There were also farmsteads at Lett Lane (now School Road), Moor Green Lane, Springfield Road and Low Lane (Stoney Lane).

Small cottages occupied by rural labourers nestled on Billesley and Cotton Lanes, as well as more prestigious properties like Hayfields and the Woodlands. References to these old houses are preserved in modern street names in the locality. Between Billesley Lane and St Agnes Road stood Wake Green House, with Charlton Lodge at one corner of Cotton Lane and the Grove standing between Billesley and Lett Lanes. Across the road to the Grevis Hall was the Manor House and nearby the Riddings, Moor Green House. Later in the century, there were added other large houses to those already standing. Near the vicinity of modern Belle Walk was the Anderton's Mansion and Highfield House at the top of Church Road, Kingswood (where now only the name survives as a road), Hern Hill, the Mounts and Green Hill House. On Wake Green Road, Leasowes and opposite St Mary's chapel, yet another mansion replaced an earlier property, Moseley House. It is tragic that none of these fine old houses (save Moseley Hall) have come down to us from these periods.

The eighteenth century saw many developments in the village. Its pleasant rural charm began to attract the attention of successful business men from Birmingham, seeking residence away from the industrial smoke and smells from the 'the workshop of the world'. Matthew Boulton himself leased the Sarehole site where there had been a corn mill since medieval times. Boulton used this site from 1756-1761 for the rolling of sheet metal.

Development of the village progressed during this century and a number of schools were opened in the area. One of these was run by Mr and Mrs Halford at Wake Green in 1767. Miss Henrietta Johnson advertised the opening of her boarding school in 1769 for the reception of young ladies. The school was 'pleasantly situated on Cannon Hill' and she praised the area for its 'very fine, healthful air'. Mr Lander, in 1787, opened an academy close to the chapel on the Turnpike Road, and Reverend Hobson founded his school in Balsall Heath, but this was torched by a mob during the 1791 Riots. These were the beginnings of private education in Moseley, and more schools were to be established as time went by.

In this era, Moseley had its own officials who sat as Justices of the Peace at the Magistrates' Courts, and sessions were often held at the Fox and Dogs or the Fighting Cocks Hotel

Crime had by now become a bigger problem in the area and the houses of the wealthier villagers were regularly targeted by burglars, sometimes operating in gangs, prompting one newspaper to print that 'The inhabitants of Moseley and Balsall Heath have lately been annoyed by a gang of robbers, who have broken into their outhouses.' Where villains were caught, reports of their crimes were very often printed in *Aris's Birmingham Gazette*, as was the following:

> [Monday 24 December 1753] Committed to Warwickshire gaol, Edward Higgins, on suspicion of breaking into the house of Lawrence Jacob of Moseley in July or August last. Stealing £7 in money, 7 pairs of cock-heels and a pair of plated spurs, a flitch and a half of bacon…

Part of the latter was recovered from the defendant's house, along with a quantity of other valuables from similar robberies in Yardley and out near Bromsgrove. Edward Higgins was sentenced to transportation in March 1754.

There was as yet no police force as we know it, but the King's Heath and Moseley Association for the Apprehension of Felons would appear to have been set up in May 1797. This body placed regular advertisements in the aforementioned gazette announcing the following incentives:

> We, whose names are here underwritten, being members of the said association, do agree to give the following rewards to any person through whose information any offender shall be brought to justice and convicted. For any person convicted of a capital offence, the sum of £6.6 shillings. For every person that shall be sentenced to be transported the sum of £4.4 shillings. For every person convicted of a less crime, the sum of £2.2 shillings. For every Toll Gatekeeper who shall give information of any Horse-Stealer, Highway-Robber, or any person who shall have stolen any cattle or sheep, or any House-Breaker, so that he, she, or they may be apprehended, the sum of one guinea.

Similar appeals were made by private individuals when a reward could be offered, and likewise printed in the local papers in hope of bringing miscreants to justice. These appeals seem to go back quite some way.

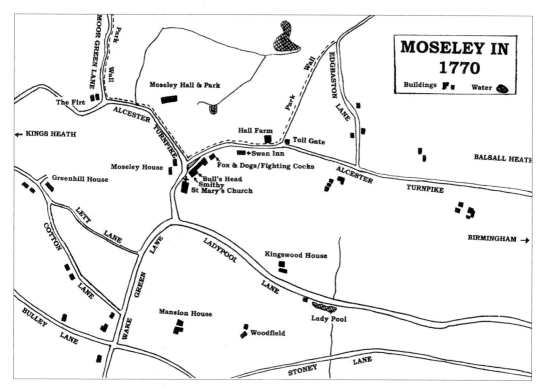

Map, 1770.

[14 December 1777] Lost from Moseley Birmingham, four sheep, three small ones raddled down the shoulder all notched on each side of the hip. Whoever will give intelligence of them so that they might be had again shall be handsomely rewarded, and have all reasonable charges paid, by applying to Mr Burton, Butcher, or Mr Smith, Fox and Dogs Moseley.

The Fighting Cocks, as the name suggests, was the venue for what must have been the most popular sport of the period. The enthusiasm for cock-fighting appealed to all social classes and many contests were geographically based affairs, as was the event recorded as taking place at the Fighting Cocks on 26 December 1759, between the gentlemen of Warwickshire and Worcestershire. Thirty cocks (fifteen each side) fought it out 'for two guineas a battle'. It was a tournament-style contest by process of elimination, the main prize being £10. The cocks would fight in a ring and were carefully paired by weight, much the same way present-day boxers are.

There were, however, no such regulations at this time for bare-knuckle pugilists, who often tore one another to shreds for prize money. The cocks were very often fitted with sharp bone or metal spurs strapped over their own, thus insuring a fight to the death. Cock fighting enjoyed widespread popularity until the Royal Society of Cruelty to Animals enforced the 1835 Act against such sports.

Not all wagers involved blood-letting, however, (although what were considered the best ones probably did), for in Aris's *Birmingham Gazette* of 15 January 1759 it was announced that George Guest, 'a Waggoner', had laid a bet that he could walk a thousand miles in twenty-eight days, 'which is upwards of thirty-five miles a day'. Mr Guest began his walk on Moseley Wake Green but covered only thirty-one miles that day, 'but every day since he's walked the full number and it is thought by many that he will win his wager'.

By 29 January the same source declared:

On Friday at six o'clock George Guest finished the walking of one thousand miles. He had one hundred and six miles to walk in the last two days with so little fatigue that he walked six miles in the last hour and had until noon to do it in.

For a very brief period, entertainment was to be enjoyed at the Moseley Theatre, which was built in 1777, entirely of wood. It stood on the Alcester Road in Balsall Heath until it was burnt down the following year.

In 1767, the Alcester Turnpike was established, but a tollgate was not erected in Moseley until 1801. This was sited at the junction of present-day Park Hill and Alcester Road, just opposite Hall Farm, which then stood along the park wall boundary.

A typical land agreement document of the eighteenth century. This one concerns the purchase of land in King's Heath in the parish of King's Norton, by victualler John Groves of Moseley, from Samuel Adams. It is signed and dated 8 January 1778.

St Mary's church as it was during the eighteenth century. The ancient cottages, seen here within the church wall, existed until 1871 when they were demolished in favour of the front section of the churchyard. To the left, a gentleman is strolling past the John Murray buildings, which were erected in 1789 and still survive.

Here the road was roughly forty-yards wide, with its centre deeply furrowed by hundreds of years of traffic and bad weather. This formed a 'holloway', so that it sat well below the level of the surrounding land. Moseley's soil, however, is strong and was not given to the to the wear of other toll roads, such as the one at Deritend, whose soft clay had been rutted to a depth of about forty-feet below the general area.

The Tollhouse keeper kept warm within the lodge and emerged at eight-thirty each morning to open the barrier gate for the Alcester coach and to stop other traffic for payment. The tariff was one shilling for a six-horse coach and a penny for a horseman. Vehicles of other descriptions were reckoned somewhere in between. The gatekeeper was given strict instructions to report all owners whose carriages or wagons were teamed by a greater number of horses than was permitted by act of parliament, and these people faced prosecution.

This road improved travelling between Alcester and Birmingham immensely, and as a result, further expansion ensued along the Turnpike from Highgate. To some degree the road compensated for the lack of a canal system, an undoubted factor, which inhibited any large-scale industrial development of Moseley during this period.

By the time of the Enclosure Act of 1772, only a small amount of waste remained common with most farmland being enclosed in fields. Allocation was thenceforth granted to owners and proprietors within that parcel of the manor. Land was generously allocated for the building of more roads and these soon began to spread across the landscape. Moor Green Road was cut through to King's Norton and another through Wake Green led to Yardley, whilst the formerly sleepy Edgbaston Lane became a public road and highway.

We know of the names of at least two of the village publicans in this period. The landlord of the Bull's Head was Thomas Blakemore, who himself owned land, and John Strettsill of the Swan Inn, who rented this premise, which stood opposite the original Grevis Hall near modern-day Chantry Road. The inn came with gardens, pasture and meadows. Sandwiched between these two alehouses were the Fox and Dogs, later to be the Fighting Cocks. Likely, each of the village landlords brewed their own beer.

During the 1770s, the oldest remaining village residence was built, this being 25 St Mary's Row, which was erected in front of the old smithy. The adjoining houses, numbers 27-31, were built for John Murray in 1789. The last house adjoins the front of the churchyard. Beyond this, until demolition sometime prior to 1871, there stood two old cottages, one end fronting onto the present pavement, breaching the church wall along St Mary's Row. These extended back towards the chapel, over what is now the pathway, leading to the main entrance beneath the bell tower. One of these was the home of the Parish Clerk. Tall trees growing here separated the cottages from John Murray's buildings. Further up the Row, near the junction of Ladypool and Wake Green Lanes, stood the previously mentioned house, Elmshurst.

THREE

The Nineteenth Century

From Pasture to Pavement

Early in the nineteenth century, there was a steady swell in the village population, with an increasing number of people coming in to settle from Birmingham. They brought with them their trades, adding further to the self sufficiency of village life, although since the establishment of the Turnpike Road outside trade was nearer at hand than ever, as were the services of 'travelling journeymen'. By 1811, the number of households in Moseley was estimated at 191, with a population of around 400. Many of the timber-framed houses, although still standing, were by now encased in the modern brickwork of the Georgian period and further small cottages were built along the country lanes.

By 1875, social segregation had become evident in Moseley, with the most affluent and successful people occupying the large houses in Moor Green, like Highbury, Pitmaston and Moor Green Hall. Next, were those who lived in the opulent premises along Wake Green Road with their spacious grounds, stables and coalhouses accessed via long and sometimes winding driveways.

After Park Hill and Chantry Roads came into existence, they formed something of a buffer between Moseley and Balsall Heath. These consisted of some very fine large Victorian and Edwardian homes, which were not perhaps affordable to the residents living on the former Blayney, Anderton and Taylor estates. It was in the village itself, however, that the lower echelons resided; the tradesmen and women who lived above or worked behind the shops, quietly plying their trades from the hidden alleyways and terraces off Woodbridge Road and St Mary's Row. Finally, there were the residents of the smaller condensed villas on Farquhar, Tudor, Leighton Roads and the many off-shoots from these and homes built later, up towards the top of Welches' Hill.

Interestingly, towards the latter part of the century, some 75% of properties in Moseley were not owned outright but were rented. The majority of owner-occupied properties were in Park Hill, Trafalgar Road and along Wake Green Road.

Population growth in the area may be charted by consulting the trade directories and the census returns for this period. The earliest directories naturally refer to Moseley as 'a village but two and a half miles distant from Birmingham' and the only residents listed are those of the upper class. By 1888, not only is Moseley referred to as a suburb but the names of most households are also given.

A hand-coloured postcard of the Marcus Ward Series. This shows The Friends Institute on Moseley Road. The building was a gift to the city from the Cadbury family and today is home to some forty-four small arts community organizations. The postcard was sent to Miss Cook of Station House Stafford on 1 August 1905. The message reads, 'Dear Miss Cook, Forgive me, I could not write before. It was nice of you to send me a card. I will write and tell you about Herr Foerster. I went to see him off. Yours very sincerely Amy Turner.'

In 1840, the village had only two shops, a butcher and a grocer. There was a resident tailor and two boot/shoemakers but they did not operate from shop premises. Other inhabitants were agricultural labourers employed on any of the eight farms around the area, those in the building trade and village inns, and not forgetting, of course, the blacksmith and his helpers.

Some twenty-seven years later in 1867, the Birmingham Post Office Directory listed fourteen premises under its commercial section for the village, as follows: 'Chemist 1, Grocers 3, Draper 1, Confectioner 1, Fishmonger 1, Butcher 1, Haberdasher 1, Newsvendor 1, Fruiterer 1, Publicans 3.'

These figures and other varieties of trade continued to rise as the century progressed and by 1896 there were about twenty different outlets about the village, including a bank. The primary landowner in the village during the mid-nineteenth century was John Taylor II of Moseley Hall. According to the Tithe Apportionments for the Yield of Moseley in 1843, he owned 938 acres. Other major landowners were Isaac Anderton, who owned 596 acres between Stoney Lane and present-day Oakland Road; Robert Mynors, who had 582 acres; George Attwood, who had 533 acres; and William Russell — once MP for east Worcestershire — who had 336 acres. His estates included what are now Pitmaston Court, Highbury, and Moorcroft Road. His name is memorialised

Moseley and Balsall Heath Institute (Moseley Road), built in 1883, was sometimes referred to as the 'Town Hall of Moseley'. Either side of the entrance within roundels are the busts of Shakespeare and Michelangelo, reflecting the building's connection with the arts. This picture was taken *c.* 1910. The building is now a Muslim community centre.

in Russell Road. Dyott was another early 1800s landowner, who still has a road named after him.

Robert Blaney owned land that lay in the fields south of St Mary's Row on both sides of present Woodbridge Road, then Blaney Street. The Tithe map of 1840 is of interest for several reasons, not least because by it we have a hearkening back to earlier Anglo-Saxon times in the names 'Hundreds' and 'Big Hundreds Meadows'. Five Lands House, now the veterinary practice, is our sole reminder of the old Open Field System, when the land here consisted of five strips.

With the establishment of 'national schools' in the early 1800s, the children of poorer families could at least receive a basic education. These schools were funded by the Anglican Church, and local landowners donated the necessary land for them to be built on. In Moseley, the Reverend Walter Farquhar Hook of St Mary's formed a committee with local gentry, including James Taylor (of Moseley Hall), William Russell, Thomas Salmon and Isaac Anderton, with the intention of building a National School in Moseley. This was completed at a cost of £465 and erected on a quarter acre of land, on Lett Lane (now School Road), leased from James Taylor. The lease was for a ninety-nine year period at one guinea per annum. It opened on Easter Day 1828 and functioned until its closure in 1969, when a new school was built further down on the corner of Oxford Road.

The upper middle class would have had their children educated privately at any of the many facilities available in the area for this purpose. These private institutions were so plentiful, that even after the Education Act was passed in 1870, no boarding schools were built in the district. There was keen competition between these establishments, who advertised in the local papers.

One such typical example was Bank House School which offered a:

... sound modern education at moderate inclusive fees. Individual attention given to backward pupils and a special class for very young boys. Principles Mr Albert S. W. Niblett, 5 years modern language Master in Hanover and Paris. Mr Alfred Niblett, Medallist and exhibitioner in natural science. Half term commences June 19th. Private pupils prepared for various examinations.

Others included Lonsdale House, Kingsley House in Coppice Road and Aubyn House at the corner of Trafalgar and Alcester Roads. Popular for young ladies was Moseley College, The Vale, and Hildathorpe in Park Hill. For boys there was Woodrough School at 36 School Road, which was eventually demolished to accommodate the Church of England Primary School.

Until 1774, Balsall Heath consisted of some 2,000 acres of empty wasteland. By the end of the 1820s, this was laid out linking Pershore Road to the Alcester Trunk Road. Between 1833 and 1835, numerous streets, all lined with cheaply built houses, sprung up between Alcester Road and Ladypool Lane. As Balsall Heathland started to disappear under a network of streets, roads and houses, so Moseley village gradually began to suffer. The encroachment of Birmingham's ever-expanding suburbia brought with it many of the social ills of the day, including typhoid epidemics, which spread from neighbouring Balsall Heath. The maladies of Moseley's poorer neighbour were so severe that as early as the 1860s, the Balsall Heath Sanitary Board was established to try and deal with its many problems, which it struggled with until the suburb was eventually annexed by Birmingham in 1891. There were sewage floods in Ladypool Lane in 1870 that contaminated the milk of local farms, spreading typhoid once again. However, the scarlet fever epidemic of 1896 was more than likely home grown, being linked to refuse tips on the Wake Green Road. Although the poor of Moseley were, in comparison, few and far between, the village came under the Poor Law Union of King's Norton, along with Balsall Heath, Edgbaston, Northfield, Harborne, Beoly and Smethwick. The passing of the Poor Law Amendment Act in 1834 gave the go-ahead for the formation of these parish unions and the building of more dreaded workhouses, as a way of frightening all but the most desperate poor into self sufficiency. These cold, grey, prison-like establishments, which stripped poor wretches of the last vestiges of dignity, catered only for those positively unable to support themselves: the maimed, infirm and the aged.

The Quarter Sessions of the early nineteenth century, as ever, cast light on a number of the problems some of the villagers were having at this time. At the Michaelmas sessions in 1809, Sarah Harrison of Moseley, the wife of John Harrison, a carpenter, testifies that she 'found William Lawrence, a stranger in her back kitchen', apparently in possession of a handkerchief, which she recognised as belonging to her lodger, Elizabeth Villars. Sarah sprung into action 'seizing his bundle' (sounds painful!) and called out for her

Moseley Art School on Moseley Road is here pictured in the early 1900s. It was the work of architect W. H. Bidlake and built in 1899, as one of the first schools which trained artists to work as designers for manufacturing. Although it is now a Grade II listed building, it has fallen into disrepair.

lodger's servant, Elizabeth Saxelby, and together they 'secured Lawrence'. Elizabeth Saxelby, spinster, also identified various other items that belonged to her mistress.

At the Michaelmass Sessions in 1814, Thomas Slater, a Moseley farmer, says that 'Enoch Milley drove his fowls, killed one, hid it under his hat and then in the hedge.'

Francis Timmins, housekeeper to John Bourne of Moseley, gave evidence at the Michaelmass Sessions on New Year's Day in 1817 that 'people came to her to ask for water and one penny of gooseberries, then for hyssop and mint'. She heard footsteps at the back of the house and was asked by Ann Guest if she had lost any pewter, as she had seen men in possession of some disperse. Upon checking she found that three pieces were missing. Thomas Freeman reported hearing 'stop thief!' out on the street and managed to apprehend Joseph Elwell and John Davis.

The same year, in 1817, a Birmingham man, Charles Tuckett, decided to take a trip to Moseley Green, to see a review of the 15th Regiment of Light Dragoons, during which his pocket was picked. He managed to seize the thief, Benjamin Edwards, 'who threw the stolen handkerchief behind him' (there seems to have been something about handkerchiefs at this time). Tuckett gave the miscreant over into the custody of D. Brownall, keeper of the prison in Aston.

As in the last century, *Aris's Birmingham Gazette* continued to print appeals for information:

[3 July 1824] Offer of £5 reward for information as to the killing of a Dane Carriage dog on Saturday 3rd. The dog belonged to Mrs Parker and was found dead under the south-west corner of the park wall.

Another local appeal for information was printed in January of the same year, under the headline 'Moor Green Body Found': 'Whereas the body of a man, about 70 years of age has been found... in a pit at Moor Green on Friday January 9th...'

There followed a very meticulous description of clothing and physical details, including the fact that he had 'lost greatest part of his front teeth and the sight in his left eye'.

The article concluded that *'The body has not yet been identified, and lies for inspection at the Bulls Head.'*

Reference to the area's rich source of both clay and gravel are apparent in the following newspaper announcements:

[16 November 1801] On Monday last, a man and a boy getting gravel out of a pit at Moseley, impudently undermined too far, several ton of earth in an instant fell upon them, and both their lives were lost.

[17 March 1845] Bully Lane to be sold freehold Cottage-Land 'AN EXCELLENT MINE OF CLAY'

Then, as now, the public were always eager to hear gossip and the closer to home the better. Two of the most relished local scandals of the late nineteenth century were the trials of George Woodyatt Hastings and Henry Beresford Moore, which were both separate cases involving fraud.

On 1 August 1889, it was announced that Henry Beresford Moore, of The Firs, Trafalgar Road, and known as 'Moseley Baronet', was committed for trial on charges of fraud and theft. In 1892, George Woodyatt Hastings, an M.P. of the House of Commons, fell from an even greater height when he was charged with the fraudulent appropriation of over £20,000 from an estate in his trust. He was expelled from the Commons and sentenced to five years' penal servitude.

Entertainment & Leisure

Given the prosperity of a high proportion of local people during the late-Victorian era, anything on which a wager could be placed was acceptable. I have already given mention to cock fighting due to its popularity in the eighteenth century, but there is reference to it as early as 1603, as noted by Everson, when 'Walter Rotton of Moseley, a man given to many extravagances, as cock-fighting and dicing soon put an end to his estate.' There were also dog fights and bare-knuckle bouts arranged, by which a handsome purse could be won — or lost. One such event is given mention in the *Birmingham Chronicle* as taking place at Wake Green, Moseley, on 26 January 1821, when Ben Preston and Bill Goold squared up to one another. Both were described as lightweights, 'neither being more than 10 stone 7lbs' and unknown to the ring, although both 'had dabbled a little

Above and below: As the population of Moseley increased during the nineteenth century, a wide variety of arts and leisure clubs began to spring up across the district. These pictures show members of one of them: Newton Lawn Tennis Club.

in the art... they were mere infants to the science'. The fight, we are assured, was most enthusiastically attended.

The military turnouts at Wake Green often drew a lot of attention. Such an occasion was in August 1807, when the third battalion of the Loyal Birmingham Volunteers marched there to receive Colonel Sir Grey Skipwith, and there were other occasions, such as when James Taylor, who had served as a captain in the Queen's Own Worcestershire Yeomanry, entertained the King's Norton Troop when he opened his hall gardens for a banquet on the annual Waterloo Day celebrations.

As the population continued to grow, so did the demand for more organised leisure activities and outlets for ladies, gentlemen and families. Birmingham, with its theatres and music halls, was but a short coach or train ride away, but there was more than enough local talent and interest for the formation of a wide range of clubs and societies. These included the Moseley Amateur Drama Society (founded in 1882), Moseley Shakespearian Society, Moseley Choral Society (founded in 1886), Moseley Musical Society, Moseley and Balsall Heath Literary Association (recorded in 1877) and a local photographic society (which appears to have died a death in 1899 due to apathy).

There were also numerous sporting associations, like the Moseley & Balsall Heath Cricket Club, which was established during the mid-1850s and the Moseley Cricket

This view, looking down what was to become St Mary's Row, shows the centre of the village as it was in 1877. The green is still but a patch of grass and in the distance can be seen the wall of the Moseley Hall estate. The remains of the gatepost beneath the tree in the left of the foreground belong to Moseley House, which stood opposite the church.

Club, founded in 1864. Moseley Football Club was founded in 1870, and Moseley Golf Club opened at Billesley Hall Farm in 1892. Moseley Park Lawn Club is recorded as holding its first annual tournament in 1886 at the Reddings, and Moseley Harriers winning the Cross Country Championships every year from 1881-1884. Moseley Ladies Cycling Club was formed in 1896 and both a working men's club and a working girls' club in 1886. The Moseley and Kings Heath Gentleman's Club opened in 1893. There was even a Moseley Book Club, and the village had its own publication in the founding of the *Moseley Society Journal* in 1891.

Shortly after the turn of the twentieth century, a ladies' hockey club was formed in 1909, a Gentleman's Swimming Club in 1911 and Moor Green Football Club in 1906 when the members of Ashfield Cricket Club decided to keep active during winter by kicking a ball about. The Prince of Wales, not content with a darts team, also had its own shooting club just prior to the First World War. Private functions and dances were held at the Moseley and Balsall Heath Institute, which was founded in 1876, and from 1883, sited where the ornate building remains to this day on the Moseley Road, Balsall Heath. The King's Heath Institute, which stood on the site of present-day Woolworths on the High Street, was another outlet. From at least 1860, there were horticultural shows and later still, Moseley Botanical Gardens was another venue.

The old Toll Gate House stood on Alcester Road at the top of Park Hill until 1872 when it was demolished. The Texaco Petrol Station now occupies its space.

This large old property stood close-by the Toll House opposite Park Hill and was probably amongst the houses bombed during the Second World War, and it was later cleared for the building of Park Hill Junior School.

For the less prosperous villagers there was the pleasure ground, which opened behind the Fighting Cocks after its partial rebuild in 1861. This included a bowling green, which was replaced by a bandstand in 1880, and in-turn by King Edward Road when that was laid through in 1901. A further venue of entertainment was provided in 1912, with King's Heath's first cinema, and a second followed in 1914. That same year, Balsall Heath's was built but, of course, the many literary minded of Moseley preferred a good book. For these there was the Moseley Book Club, as has been mentioned. A library had been established in the village in 1894 and there were also at least two booksellers. With cinemas in both Kings Heath and Balsall Heath, what need did Moseley have for its own cinema? For this reason the locals fought moves to have one built within the village, and besides, it 'kept the riff-raff out!'

A skating rink was opened in 1875 and sited just behind the Trafalgar Inn. Skating was a very popular activity and there were several other venues for this during the winter season. One of these was undoubtedly the new Moseley Pool, which opened in 1894 at Swanshurst Park, close by the corner of Coldbath Road and Swanshurst Lane; it was initially opened for use of fishing and boating clubs. Nearby Coldbath Pond was also used for skating, but the main venue was, of course, on the Moseley Hall estate when the park stood behind the stone walls and lodge gates. This was before the pool was severed from the grand old mansion by Salisbury Road and the parade of shops erected. Admission was charged and half the money raised went to charity, as was the case in February 1895. The whole of one Sunday's takings of £12 5s 6d went towards relief of the distressed of the district, and eventually, more than £1,000 was taken at the gates — such was the popularity of skating. There were, of course, mishaps and one of these occurred a month prior, on 5 January 1895, on the first day of admissions. A large crowd of skaters enthusiastically headed out onto the ice. One of them, a Miss Cross of Crompton Road, Handsworth, was blissfully skating hand-in-hand with her brother around the pond when suddenly the ice gave way beneath them and they plunged down into twenty feet of freezing water together. Fortunately, the lad retained tight grip of his sister's hand and, with the other, clung to the edge of the broken ice, keeping their heads above the water until rescue arrived. One end of a coat was thrown to him and when he clutched this, the pair was held firm and a ladder brought to the scene. Miss Cross, who had immediately lost consciousness, was carried to the gates and conveyed in a cab to the residence of friends in Ascot Road. Meanwhile, her brother, who played for Moseley Football club, was taken over to the Fighting Cocks Hotel, where he dried off and was given a change of clothes before being able to return home. Miss Cross was to remain in Ascot Road some days before she was fit enough to go home, and once there, she took to her bed for several more days in a very critical condition. News of the accident was initially kept from their mother, who was just recovering from a severe illness.

The celebration of national events was organised by local committees, who raised the necessary money. Such was the case in 1837, on the occasion of Queen Victoria's Coronation when a banquet was held for the National School pupils and members of the poorer adult population. The Queen's Own Regiment of Worcestershire Yeomanry paraded on Wake Green, and a three-round salute followed by hearty cheers was sounded before the soldiers tucked into an English breakfast, served up to them 'by their two lieutenants and coronet'.

James Taylor of Moseley Hall was personally presented to the new Queen the following month at a royal levee, so no doubt many in Moseley were later to receive a first-hand account as to the personality and appearance of Her Majesty.

Queen Victoria made a flying visit through the village in 1843. On 10 August, *The Times* reported:

> The precise time of Her Majesty's arrival in Birmingham was not generally known, but notwithstanding, in the neighbourhood of Moseley and King's Norton a considerable number of the most respectable inhabitants were assembled along the banks and bridges of the railway, and gave the Queen as she passed a most hearty reception.

If records were kept on some of the other national celebrations of these former times, it seems they have not survived. The occasion of Victoria's golden jubilee in 1887 does, however, receive a mention in the village annals, for £170 was reported to have been raised to spend on meals for some 5,000 children of the village, as well as the aged poor. Ten years later, £250 was spent on the celebration of the Queen's diamond jubilee, when all the children marched in procession to a meadow at Moor Green for sporting activities and a meal, whilst the elderly ate theirs at home.

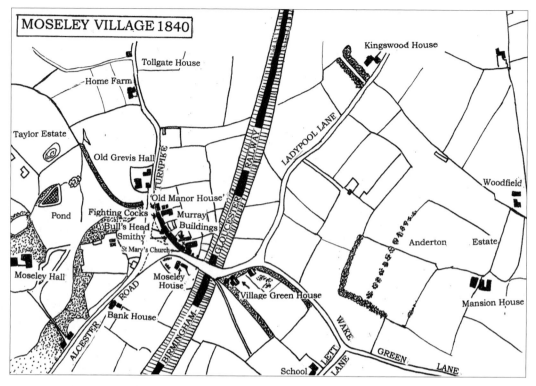

Map, 1840.

The shops along the High Street were richly decked out for the event, prompting the *Moseley Society Journal* to remark:

> In a small way Moseley took part in the celebrations. Festoons and bunting made the appearance bright and pleasing to the eye. Tradesmen near the green and church made the loyalist show of the day. The tranquil repose of the green was broken in the afternoon to witness the procession of school children who to the strength of over 600, representing St Mary's Day and Sunday Schools, and Oxford Road Sunday School. Having sung the national anthem on the green, the procession reformed and wended its way to a large meadow adjoining Moor Green, placed at the disposal of the committee by Mr Richard Cadbury... the little inmates of the Moseley Hall Convalescence Home were not forgotten. The interior of the building was bravely decorated with flags. Two fine trees were planted in the gardens by the youngest and eldest child and others lustily sang the national anthem. Special tea was supplied by the ladies and Amusement Committee, and Mrs Heaven of Chantry Road gave each child a medal. Coloured fires were lit and balloons sent up in the evening and each child was given a toy.

On 6 August 1902, an announcement was made that the Residents of King's Heath and Moseley Traders Association had agreed to combine the festivities and celebrations

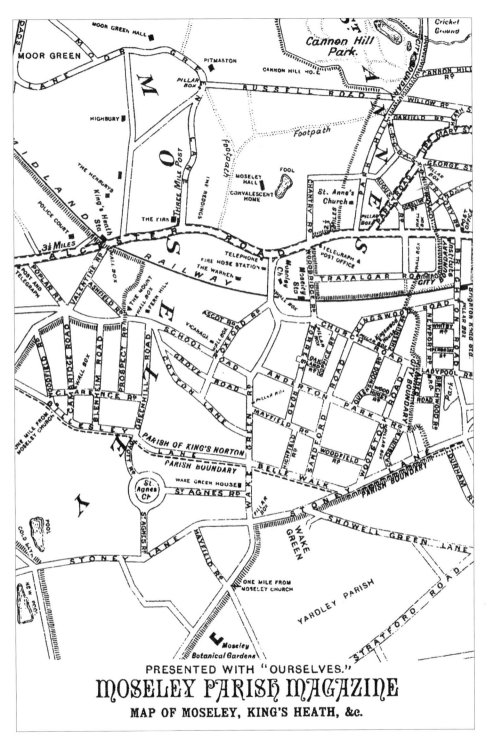

PRESENTED WITH "OURSELVES."

MOSELEY PARISH MAGAZINE

MAP OF MOSELEY, KING'S HEATH, &c.

Map, 1893.

to mark the Coronation of the new King, Edward VII, and that preparations were under way for a street parade on the Saturday morning, which would include three bands accompanied by parties of veterans, Naval Brigade and Imperial Yeomanry, in procession from King's Heath to Moseley and back again to King's Heath. 'Those who have vehicles are requested to place them at the disposal of the committee as early as possible.'

Earlier, between 1 and 2 June 1902, there were some unofficial celebrations which it might be appropriate here to make mention of, this being the end of the Boer War. One local newspaper carried the story of one such celebration this way:

The official news of the declaration of peace was rather late in arriving in King's Heath and Moseley on Saturday night. A few stray copies of 'Specials' found their way to the suburbs between 8 and 9, but the official announcement was not posted at King's Heath post office until between 9 and 10. The juvenile portion of the place led the way in rejoicing, parading the streets beating tins and cheering. Later as news began to be circulated, hundreds assembled on High Street. Backyards were ransacked for anything that would burn, and very soon a bonfire was blazing on the corner of York and Alcester Roads. Rockets and crackers were let off and shortly after, members of King's Heath Lamplighters Brass Band arrived and played patriotic airs. Towards midnight the crowds headed towards Highbury shouting themselves hoarse in cheering Mr Chamberlain and vocalising the strains of the National Anthem, interspersed with snatches of 'Soldiers of the Queen,' 'Dolly Gray,' and other popular melodies.

Gas lighting came to Moseley in 1877. Twenty-one years later, the use of electricity was to become a reality, when the *Moseley Society Journal* announced in June 1898:

The King's Norton District Council applies for power to possess electric light and the Board of Trade has issued copies of a new provincial order which they have just issued to the Rural District Council of King's Norton authorising them to supply electricity for all public and private purposes.

Although this implied that the supply of electricity to the Moseley area was imminent, it was evidently quite some time in arriving in any scale. The same source, in its August 1911 issue, states:

The City of Birmingham Electric Supply Department, realizing the demand for current in the Moseley area, have not been content to wait for the actual annexation of Moseley, but by arrangement with King's Norton Urban District Council, have already prepared to give a supply of electricity to the Moseley area. This supply, which was commenced about the middle of September, is at present given from a sub-station situated within the existing city boundary. Current can be given, if required in the following roads:- Salisbury Road, Reddings Road, Russell Road, Parkhill, Park Road, Chantry Road, Edgbaston Road, Augusta Road, Trafalgar Road, St Mary's Row, part of Oxford Road, and Alcester Road. It is hoped that by next season sub-stations will be erected in King's Heath and Showells Green districts, and from these sources a supply will be given to practically the whole of the Moseley area.

The general quality of Moseley water at the close of the nineteenth century was well known. It came from both deep wells and natural springs, which may, or may not, have been the source of supply for the Moseley Mineral Water Company, which operated suspiciously for some years from one of the back courts in Highgate. The origin of their produce may more likely have been the Rea. None the less, 'Moseley Mineral Water' was marketed and sold in its own very distinctive looking glass bottles, which carried the name of the company and its motif, a crowing cockerel.

For a very short time, it seems Moseley had its own fire brigade, which was formed in 1897 and installed in premises that were erected, so says the *Moseley Society Journal*, 'near Mr Bullock's house'. The station was equipped with 'a fire escape, hose cart and Toziers patent hand engine and kept there with several hundred feet of hose'.

Over the next couple of years, the Moseley Fire Brigade, operating as a branch of King's Heath Fire Brigade (based in Silver Street), attended a number of fires around the village. However, after some friction with the parent branch, which culminated in the withholding of a Long Service Medal from one Lieutenant Seeley, the Moseley Fire Brigade resigned and the village was, at least for some time, dependant upon King's Heath and Lime Grove stations for fire extinction.

At least three blazes, which the Moseley Fire Brigade attended, were recorded in the local journal:

[October 1897] An alarming fire broke out last month at Uffculme, the beautiful residence of Mr Richard Cadbury, JP at Moor Green Lane. Its seat was in the cellar, and was caused by the fusion of wires conveying electric currents for the lighting of the house. The fire was speedily got under control by the efforts of Mr Cadbury and family, who brought hand pumps and other fire extinguishing apparatus to bear upon the flames.

[May 1898] The Moseley Fire Brigade have had frequent calls to fires of late. On 26th February they were called to a blaze in the Woodbridge Road, where the shop window of Miss Lloyd, milliner, was well alight. The fire was put out before their arrival. They had another call at midnight on March 4th, to a house in Caroline Road, where the servant girl, who was in the habit of reading in bed, had gone to sleep with the candle burning,

The Population of Moseley During the Nineteenth Century

This may be gauged, at least during the earlier period, by the number of recorded households. In 1811, as previously mentioned, there were 191 and by 1840 the number had increased to 380.

The figures of the census returns enable us to see with a little more accuracy the actual population, and these are reflected in the figures below.

1861 1,491
1871 2,374
1881 4,232
1891 7,210

Longevity

Doubtless, the clean Moseley air and surroundings contributed greatly to the many instances of longevity in the area, for it is interesting to note that between 1800 and 1850 no less than ten villagers lived beyond ninety years. This was at a time when the average life expectancy was between thirty-seven and forty-five years, depending on environment. Furthermore, another forty-four Moseley inhabitants lived into their eighties and seventy-eight died between their seventieth and eightieth birthday. As sanitation and public health in general improved, it naturally followed that life expectancy increased also, and there are several references in the *Moseley Society Journal* of locals reaching a goodly age.

Mr William Hawkes of Caroline Road was one centenogerian. He was born in Norwich in 1794, moved to Moseley in 1868 and died here in his one-hundredth year. Mrs Grove died in 1811 at the age of ninety-two.

The *Birmingham Mail* on 9 February 1901 carried a story about an un-named Moseley lady of ninety who had lived through the reign of five English monarchs:

> The long reign of George III, had nearly ten years to run at her birth, she afterwards lived under his successor, George IV, then William IV, and the late Queen Victoria, and to-day she acknowledges as her King the newly created Edward VII.

Mrs Ann Harris of St Mary's Row, who died in 1928, was at the time Moseley's oldest resident, born 'in October 1837, in a house now destroyed, near the old Bull's Head'. She died at the home of her brother-in-law Mr Charles Cross, the ninety-one-year-old verger of St Mary's parish church, being close by her birthplace. Ann Harris 'was a daughter of Edward (Ned) Dickenson, who in the 50s-60s of the last century was beadle and clerk of Moseley Parish Church'.

Towards the end of the century, in 1894, the Moseley Paper was moved to comment:

> Moseley has a reputation of being a salubrious suburb, but judging by the large number of medical practitioners located in Moseley Road, one would suppose that it was not. From Highgate Park to the tram terminus at Moseley, a distance of about half a mile, there are nineteen doctors!

FOUR

The Early Twentieth Century
Annexation to Armistice, 1918

As far back as the 1870s, the people of Moseley had lived with the fear of annexation with Birmingham and were anxious to preserve their distinct identity and character, voicing their trepidation whenever possible. Over the next — almost — forty years, a number of meetings were convened at various dates and locations to debate this subject; the gatherings were always lively, with the vast majority of those in attendance against the proposed annexation.

Typical was one reported as taking place in April 1886 at the Skating Rink, Moseley. It was resolved that all present showed 'strong apprehension and disfavour' towards the proposal of the Birmingham authorities to include Moseley in the extension of the municipal area of the Borough of Birmingham and that they, '... being of the opinion that no good or useful purpose can be served thereby [would] pledge itself to use every legitimate means in its power to resist to the uttermost any attempt by the Birmingham authorities to carry out the above scheme, or to remove Moseley from the county of Worcester.'

It appears that for a while there existed — in some form — a Moseley and King's Heath Parliament with its own Prime Minister. Whether or not this ever achieved anything is not known, but on 11 November 1907, there was a sitting to debate a bill for limitation of credit trading between shopkeepers and the working classes, with a view to curtailing it, and on 20 November, the parliament met again to discuss the apathy amongst ratepayers but, no doubt due to apathy, the meeting was poorly attended!

There were also financial difficulties for the parliament, as one sitting highlighted the incurred deficit of £4.11s.6d, 'which was due to the adverse balance of the picnic at Hewel'.

Obviously, 'local government' being what it was, and despite the vociferous protests to the contrary, the inevitable eventually happened and the village was swallowed up by the sprawling Birmingham Corporation in 1911, along with King's Heath, King's Norton, Yardley, Sarehole and many other areas. The population of Birmingham stood at this time at around half a million, but with these annexations it almost doubled overnight. As for Moseley, with a population now at 16,806, it was no longer a fashionable and genteel Worcestershire village but had been absorbed within the vast expanding metropolis of the City of Birmingham. Balsall Heath had succumbed in 1891 and was duly rewarded with improved road, drainage, street lighting and refuse collection, a fire service and public park. There was also the addition of the present-day (albeit now somewhat dilapidated) landmarks, such as the Moseley School of Art, the public baths, opened by the Lord Mayor in 1907, and the library which had opened earlier in 1896. Above its entrance, and incorporated in large-scale amongst the architecture, the Birmingham Corporation Arms proclaiming the motto 'Forward' to all passers by, including, and perhaps especially, those citizens still as yet un-subjugated, making their way to and from town. These grand civic buildings were erected perhaps as lures, architectural carrots on sticks or offerings to those outside the corporation, what could perhaps be theirs if they would only submit.

The population of Moseley by 1900 stood at just over 11,000, and, according to *Kelly's Directory* three years later, there were trading in the village:

Chemists 2, Bakers 2, Fishmongers 2, Grocers 8, Butchers 4, Tobacconists 3, Drapers 9, Confectioners 2, Corn Dealers 2, Book Sellers 2, Ironmongers 2, Hairdressers 2, Florists 2, Tailors 2, Dairymen 2, Builder 2, Decorator 1, Plumber 1, Newsagent 1, Dressmaker 1, Upholsterer 1, Hosier 1, Boot/Shoe Makers 4, Stationer 1, Baby Linen Specialist 1, Watchmaker 1, Umbrella Maker 1, Vet 1, Bank 1.

These figures demonstrate the demand being imposed by the rapidly increasing population, following the large-scale development in the area, which was still taking place. That Moseley was regarded as 'the place to be' if means allowed, is borne out when comparing the rateable value of the area, which was higher than any other ward. For example, in 1897, Moseley was reckoned at having a total area rateable value of £63,000, whilst Selly Oak, whose population was 20% higher, had a rateable value of only £43,000. This was at a time when it was said that there were more millionaires in Moseley than any other suburb of Birmingham. The *Birmingham Post*, in an article printed on 14 November 1901, said, in part:

There are probably few residential suburbs which have so rapidly undergone the process of transformation as Moseley. Its development during the last quarter of a century, and especially within the last decade, is remarkable, and today the place would be scarcely recognised by any old Moseleyite returning to his native place after a fairly long absence. This development is well illustrated by a wheel with many spokes, having 'Moseley Green,' as it is commonly called, for the hub. But the aspect, of the hub itself has altered, and little, if anything of a century ago remains to save...

Similarly, the editor of the *Moseley Society Journal* in 1911 expressed the same sentiments when he lamented:

Within the last twenty years the hand of the builder has made ruthless onslaughts in Moseley. Many residents can remember when the suburb was just a delightful retreat from the noise and care of the city and its whirl. Now with the march of latter-day progress, it has become a continuation of, rather than apart from, the city and noise.

Indeed, now just as then, it is sobering to ask, 'At what cost has all this development been achieved?' Whilst doubtless many would be proud of the benefits, improvements

A man in stocks in Moseley. Unfortunately, the message on the reverse of this postcard, which was posted from the village on 18 February 1909, offers no further clues as to what it is all about. Maybe an earlier form of village idiot competition?

and progress brought about by all this expansion, it has all been at great cost of the environment, which has been robbed of so much rural beauty and tranquillity. The peace and scenic serenity of Moseley village, the virtues for which it was once so coveted, first by farmer then by businessman, retired professional and artisan alike, these proved to be the means to its own end.

The First World War

With the outbreak of the First World War, the humdrum routine life of the villagers was turned upside down, much the same as in other communities across the country, as the men folk flocked to the flag joining Kitchener's army. This included the sons of the wealthy and their menservants. Entire bodies volunteered to serve together in the 'Pals Brigades', like the men of the Ashfield Cricket Club. Various units were created locally, one being the Moseley Training Corps. Another was the Moseley Rifle Corps who by 1915, had sixty members and met on Monday and Wednesday nights, utilising the Stoney Lane Drill Hall.

There were bombing raids over the Midlands area by Zeppelins and all sectors of the community became involved in the war effort in one way or another. The Moseley Auxiliary Branch of the Birmingham Citizen's Committee organised bazaars to raise money, as well as helping the Lord Mayors' Appeal by collecting records, books and even razor blades for the fleet. Some local women trained as nurses or undertook sewing and other needlework for the military. Even the local schoolchildren did their bit (despite the fact that many of them were themselves in need of a little of charity), forming concert parties to entertain the patients in the various temporary hospitals dotted about, as well as some of the refugee hostels. There were also school collections of candles to be sent for use in the trenches and fruit for the wounded. Girls and young ladies knitted woollen socks, balaclavas and scarves for the soldiers at the front. Moseley school procured for itself the use of an allotment for the growing of vegetables during this period, from which teachers made soup for the poorest children in the colder weather, and tickets were issued for bread. Schoolchildren were very often sent home because of the lack of coal to heat the boilers.

There was an attempt in the early years of the war to maintain the regular social functions and activities that had traditionally taken place. For example, the Moseley Ladies Hockey Club still met and various musical functions and lectures were still held at the institutes, but, here again, with so many men folk away and others engaged in war work, these activities began to slide away with the progression of the war.

From the outset, travel to and from the village was affected, when in the second month of the war, the army commandeered the horses of Moseley Mews Cab Company.

Preoccupation with the war effort quite naturally saw a slow down in building in and around the village, although the present post office near the crossroads on the Alcester Road opened in 1915.

The large homes of many of the more affluent villagers were given over to the cause, providing hospital and hostel accommodation for the wounded and their visiting family members. Moor Green House, the home of Sir John Holder, was turned into a hostel for Belgian refugees and later a hospital for officers, which was staffed by local

Members of 3rd City of Birmingham Battalion Royal Warwickshire Regiment in what was once the assembly Hall of Spring Hill College, during the First World War. This postcard was issued by Arthur Wells of Moseley Road.

girls. Chamberlain's residences at Highbury also became a war hospital. Sorrento took in military casualties from 1915 and Stanley House, standing on the corner of Wake Green and Mayfield Roads, served temporarily as a hostel for Belgian refugees, as did Uffculme, whose first guests arrived in September 1914. Two years later, it was turned into a 200-bed hospital, run by the Friends Ambulance Unit after Richard Cadbury donated it to the war effort. The Dingle, Wake Green Road, was utilised by The Red Cross, and Spring Hill College was commandeered in 1914 for use as barracks for The Royal Warwickshire Regiment. This, however, was not big enough and many more men were billeted with nearby residents, and Windermere, a vacant building opposite, became officers' quarters.

As in most other churches, special services were held at St Mary's for intercessions and prayers for victory, but the choir were very much depleted and soon the names of some of them and other local men began to appear in the papers amongst the long lists of casualties, and many obituaries were printed in the church magazine.

This entire period was one of general depression and anxiety in all the lands affected by the war. Despite the propaganda inspired stories of pluck and courage, which were aimed at banding the populace together, nowhere are these feelings more reflected on the home front than in the publications of the time. War brings out an often-contagious unity and patriotism amongst ordinary people, as history itself bears witness, but it also shows that in such times of conflict it can also bring out the worst. Hitherto friendly aliens living peacefully in communities suddenly become suspected spies and undesirables in our midst. Such foreigners who ran businesses suffered particularly when their shops were shunned and the owners accused of disloyalty towards the host community and nation. In one local case, a trader, who was actually of Belgian descent, was compelled to post his birth certificate in his shop window to prove he was born in Ladywood.

Members of 3rd Battalion again, this time on parade in the college grounds 1914-18.

The opinions and assertions made locally by Mr Fred Box, editor of the *Birmingham, Moseley and King's Heath Society Journal*, undoubtedly fuelled fear and suspicion in these neighbourhoods. Sadly, his views were what we can only conclude to be the general feeling at this time.

In his November issue of 1914, shortly following the outbreak of war, Mr Box demands, beneath his section entitled 'What the editor would like to know?' is:

Why a certain tradesman in King's Heath has never put his name on the premises? Is he ashamed, or afraid to, which?

Why another German tradesman in the same district has had his name painted out from the doorway? Did the former appearance make any difference to his business?

Who made the suggestion that a certain tradesman should burn all German goods (bought before the war), and whether the proposer is prepared to compensate him if he does?

Among his narrative there were also continual references to German deviance and Hunnish atrocities, from which even dumb animals were not safe.

A fine puppy brought to England from Antwerp by a Belgian refugee is safely housed at Moor Green House, and is the pet of the guests there. It was picked up for fear of the Germans bayoneting it, as it is no uncommon sight in Antwerp to see them bayoneting poor defenceless dogs.

A Message from Moseley.

A HEAVY POST.

A Message from Moseley — A Heavy Post. No doubt some of the women who took on the postmen's rounds during the First World War were a bit big. The poor chap on this postcard looks vaguely like Neville Chamberlain. The message written in pencil on the reverse says, 'Trust this is not the only one to-day Tres Bon Ici-Cabber.' It is addressed to 'L/Cpl Billy Clayton 'C' Section 1/2 S.M. Fld Amb. B.E.F.' and was posted in Moseley at 7.45 p.m. on 3 September 1917. National Series M&L Ltd.

A group of wounded soldiers at Moor Green Hall Hospital. The patient who wrote this card in May 1917 says beneath the address, 'My new residence for the time being. Kindest Regards H.'

Whilst on the subject, although there appears to be no record of it in Moseley, 'daschund kicking' was known to have taken place at this time.

The editor's words were often also aimed at the men folk not as yet in uniform. Four months into the war he asked, 'Have all eligible young men in Moseley volunteered for army service? Or are there still a few who do not fully realise the seriousness of the job this country and its allies are engaged in?' To this end even the local clergy joined in. Rev. R. C. Lemin proudly announced in the Baptist church magazine, 'Nearly 150 of our young men are now numbered among the ranks of those who are standing for the defence of their country.'

Quoting this, Mr Box adds, 'Not much evidence of shirking there!'

As the war advanced, so too did the anti-German sentiments and praise for the 'Moseley knights in khaki'.

'He died while doing his duty.' So runs a phrase in an officer's letter of condolence to the relatives of the late Bombardier Hurle of Trafalgar Road, to which Mr Box commented:

> … and no more glorious epitaph could be bestowed upon any man. It renders all the more surprising the number of 'shirkers,' who are content to let others shoulder the task of defending England from the fate of Belgium and Poland.

In May 1918, the editor rounded on another alien, a pacifist Quaker convert who had been charged under the Defence of the Realm Act for calling for an end to the war,

Moseley Park and Pool Tennis Club c. 1930s.

saying, 'the Germans are our brothers. God didn't create man that he might kill. The war will find its quickest end when all soldiers lay down their weapons.'

Mr Box growled:

Anderton Park Road Moseley has been honoured — or shall I say dishonoured — for some time past by a Dutchman bearing the German sounding name of Boeke-Cornelius Boeke, who came to the attention of DORA. The son-in-law of Richard Cadbury turns out to be a dangerous character, recently released after serving 41 days imprisonment for making a statement likely to prejudice the administration of His Majesty's Forces. He has been sent to Holland... Anderton Park Road should smell all the sweeter now that Dutchman, as he calls himself, has been cleared out!

By the final year of the war, the editor turned his attention to other sinister threats, and there was rumour that a Bolshevik gang had established itself somewhere in Strensham Hill.

Early in 1918, some ten months before the war ended, it was proposed to erect a new church hall and parish war memorial to the local men who had lost their lives during the conflict. The commission for the memorial itself, in the form of a Calvary, was given to the Bromsgrove Guild and executed in Portland stone. This can be seen close by the churchyard gate on St Mary's Row, also the work of the Bromsgrove Guild as a memorial to Councillor Frederick Tippetts. The Lynch Gate was donated by the pupils of Wintersloe School in honour of their headmaster, Mr Fisher, in 1933 and is so inscribed. The plan to build church rooms on Oxford Road in connection with the war memorial project was quashed in the 1920s because the £4,000 bill for the necessary building work was considered too great a burden on the congregation at that time.

When the Armistice was announced in November 1918 there was rejoicing in the streets, and wounded soldiers at Moor Green House Hospital danced out on the lawns rejoicing that they were not having to go back to the front after all. Eventually, when the local servicemen did return, it was to a very different Moseley; like them, it was changed forever.

By now, Moseley had become very much part of Greater Birmingham, to which it had been drawn inexorably during the long years of war, and life in all its varied ways had altered course perpetually. The following period (the inter-war years) has been described as dull, with nothing of significance happening to alleviate the boredom of things. The villagers were now far more aware of events and circumstances taking place in the wider world outside their community. Many of the issues once of much importance to the residents — like dog licences, highway paving and street lighting, tennis players disporting themselves unbecomingly along Wake Green Road during Sunday morning church service times and the evils of flirting — previously subjects worthy of mention in the *Moseley Society Journal*, were all of little or no importance now.

FIVE

The Interwar Years

During the 1920s and 1930s, the demise of not a few men of importance to village life saw the loss or sale of their large properties as their surviving family members sold up and moved on elsewhere. For the residents who could still afford household servants, these could be difficult to come by, as many men and women had gone into the factories or other lines of trade. Added to this was the economic calamity brought about by the Wall Street crash in 1929. The resulting period of depression saw many of the large Moseley houses converted for non-residential purposes, although quite a number of these in the years to come were changed yet again, but into multiple dwellings.

Regardless, Moseley was, in this period, still a desirable place to live and continued to attract many professional people to the area. A large proportion of residents still employed servants, maids, gardeners and nannies. The maids and nannies were a common sight around the village, particularly in the private park where they would sit in a row by the pavilion chatting as they watched over the children in their charge, playing on the swings and bars.

There were still several popular private schools in the area, like St Hilda's at 123 Sandford Road, Moseley College, The Vale, Wake Green Road and Hazelwood on Prospect Road. Woodrough's in Church Road was a preparatory school for boys, and Devonshire House, Forest Road, was both a high school for girls and a kindergarten for boys, whilst Park Hill Boarding School for girls was also a prep school for boys.

Despite the Depression, village folk still found time for recreation and many of the clubs that had seen a decline during the war years began to enjoy fresh enthusiasm. Amongst these were included the Moseley Rugby Football Club and the local golf and cricket club, as well as various tennis clubs, Salisbury Bowling Club, Moseley Quoits and Bowling Club. The Moseley and Balsall Heath Institute and the Moseley and King's Heath Institute once again played host to the Moseley Musical Club and the venue for many other meetings of local interests.

To what extent the village had become more a part of the wider world is very much reflected in the *Moseley Society Journal*. Local events were mentioned scantily, whilst the troubles in Ireland, the rise of fascism in Italy, the Bolshevik take-over in Russia and the ongoing problems with Germany were very much on the editor's mind. He was to continue 'Jerry-bashing' for many years to come; ironically, this was for the remainder

of the journal's existence, which appears to have ceased in 1933, the year Hitler came to power.

In the October issue of 1923 he writes under the title 'Still Fooled by the Germans':

It is really inexplicable to the man in the street why the government allows Germany to keep on fooling them over the Ruhr question... The allies should have advanced into the heart of Germany and held Berlin!

Elsewhere in the same copy, he warned:

Hun waiters are re-appearing in large numbers in the West End Hotels and restaurants. The managers of Birmingham hotels and restaurants would be advised to turn down the dirty Hun waiter should he seek a job.

Many of his items reflected not local concerns, but, where possible, acts of heroism by local men, especially those decorated for bravery. Victoria Cross recipients, no matter from where they hailed, received particular attention in his columns, even with reference to distant appointments to various offices and positions.

In the July 1928 edition he commented:

It is interesting to state that whenever a Victoria Cross comes into the market, it always fetches a big price, in some cases fetching £100 or more. The late Mr Clarke of Ascot Road Moseley and the late Mr David Davis of Trafalgar Road were collectors of this famous decoration. The son of an old soldier who won the VC in the Zulu War 50 years ago was forced to bid in public auction last month to regain the cross for his family. It cost him £85.

The Victoria Cross here referred to was that awarded to Private Frederick Hitch.

By the mid-1930s there was a general return to prosperity, which was enjoyed for a while. During this period, many more houses were built along the Wake Green Road towards and over the Yardley Wood Road and in the direction of Sarehole. There was also continued expansion westerly, towards Cannon Hill House and Pitmaston, and by 1936, both the eastern and western sides of Salisbury Road were also completed.

SIX

The Second World War
From Appeasement to Victory

As Prime Minister of the country in 1937, Neville Chamberlain feared another terrible war with Germany. He did all he could to avert it by having dialogue with the German Fuehrer, Adolf Hitler, to discuss Germany's demands in what became known as the Munich Crisis.

Here, Chamberlain eventually obtained from the German dictator what he believed to be a guarantee that, in exchange for the disputed frontier regions of Czechoslovakia, there would be no more territorial demands on the part of Germany; at the last moment war had been avoided — or so he thought.

In jubilant mood, Chamberlain flew back to England to wave the famous 'scrap of paper' (as Hitler called it), announcing:

> My good friends, for the second time in our history, a British Prime Minister has returned from Germany bringing peace with honour. I believe it is peace in our time... Go home and get a nice quiet sleep.

Six months later, the Germans occupied the remainder of the Czechoslovakian Republic and on 1 September 1939, they invaded Poland. When demands for the withdrawal of German forces from Poland were ignored, Chamberlain once more addressed the British public to inform them that a state of war now existed between Britain and Germany.

After expressing his sorrow that none of his hard work in pursuit of peace had made any difference, he told the people:

> The Government have made plans under which it will be possible to carry on the work of the nation in the days of stress and strain which may be ahead of us. These plans need your help and you may be taking part in the fighting services or as a volunteer in one of the branches of civil defence. If so you will report for duty in accordance with the instructions you have received. You may be engaged in work essential to the prosecution of war, or in the maintenance of the life of the people in factories, in transport in public utility concerns, or in the supply of other necessaries of life. If so it is of vital importance that you carry on with your job.

Once again, as everywhere else in the country, life in Moseley Village was thrown into wartime mechanism. General mobilisation was proclaimed immediately and the evacuation of some three million women, children and invalids from the cities was undertaken at a very early stage in fear that when the air raids started, they would result in massive civilian casualties. The Air Raid Precautions that had been set up declared that 'the blackout' was to be enforced daily from sunset, whilst officers kept an eye open for visible lights from premises and fires. The air raids on the city, or 'Birmingham Blitz' as it later became known, began on 8 August 1940 and lasted until 23 April 1944.

During this period there were around 9,000 casualties recorded, including 2,241 dead, 3,010 seriously injured and 3,682 with lesser wounds. Some 12,391 homes were destroyed along with 302 factories and a further 239 buildings of other descriptions. Birmingham, because of its importance as an industrial centre, was the second most heavily bombed city outside London. During the war Government censorship insisted that raids on Birmingham were not to receive specific mention in news bulletins; rather, the target was referred to as 'a midland town'. As a result, the importance of the city in the country's war effort and the heavy devastation and suffering of its population has not always been recognised. So extensive was the damage to housing stocks during this time that it necessitated the development of a number of large housing estates across Birmingham, in a twenty-year project commencing shortly after the end of the war.

Moseley itself, being only a couple of miles from the city centre, had its fair share of bombs dropped on it*, and at one point, it seemed, according to one witness, that almost every street in the village was illuminated by blazing gas pipes! One resident of Oxford Road recalls hearing the air raid warning at around two in the afternoon. He was called outside by his father to have a look at a German bomber flying parallel with the road, low enough as to be able to distinguish the black crosses under its wings. It came under fire from anti-aircraft guns stationed in Swanshurst Park, but their shooting was too wide and the shells exploded in a triangle about it.

Many people erected 'Anderson shelters' in their back gardens or reinforced cellars if they had them. There were public shelters also, with one at the junction of Wake Green and Yardley Wood Roads, and others at Moseley Hall Hospital and Uffculme.

One woman, Carrie Constance Hinett of Windmere Road Moseley, was charged with 'committing a disorderly act in a shelter' when she and her husband made their way inside with their pet dog. The warden protested, telling them that dogs were not allowed in the shelter. Mrs Hinnett became abusive and refused to remove the dog. Police officers arrived at the scene and when a sergeant told her that if she did not remove the dog then he would personally eject it from the shelter, she screamed 'you can tell Scotland Yard if you like, you rotters!' The case against Mrs Hinett was dismissed on payment of costs.

Parishioners at St Mary's were requested to remain seated or lie down flat on the floor in the event of an air raid during service time. The church did, on several occasions, sustain bomb damage. In the October of 1940, an incendiary found its way in, presumably via the roof of the nave, and set fire to one of the pews and caused damage to one of the pillars. Had not the canon been keeping watch at the time, a lot more destruction may have occurred. Later in the year, on 3 December, a landmine exploded

---

*Balsall Heath fared worse, being an area of closely built houses and factories all mixed together.

beyond the railway line, shattering the glass of the east window, as well as those of the north and south sanctuary, the lady chapel and north aisle.

Further up the Wake Green Road at the Sorrento Maternity Hospital, the everyday running of things carried on as efficiently as possible under the circumstances. When the air raid sirens were sounded the nurses loaded babies, sometimes as many as four, in prams and wheeled them off to the shelters with mothers following behind. This sometimes led to a little confusion, as some of the mothers were later reunited with the wrong babies.

Another resident, a lad at the time, remembered living on the Yardley Wood Road until his parents got another place a short distance away. After they left, another family moved in but sadly they were killed a couple of weeks later when the house was bombed.

Almost oblivious to the dangers of war, it was often a time of great excitement for children, and boys in particular found great enjoyment in hunting for shrapnel after a raid. A nose cone was a real prize. But it was also a time of great heartache as youngsters were separated from their parents and sent into the countryside to stay with strangers for the duration. Rows of boys and girls were packed onto the platform at Moseley station, all wearing name-tags and carrying satchels and gasmasks, bound for an often unknown destination.

During the Second World War, Moseley was not immune to bomb damage, and a number of properties were damaged or destroyed. This house stood on the south side of Woodbridge Road immediately before the railway bridge itself, which can be seen just behind the lamppost.

This house on Bloomfield Road was another which was totally destroyed.

Schools at these locations had to be shared. For instance, Moseley shared Harry Cheshire School in Kidderminster. They had their lessons in the morning and then cleared out their desks before the Moseley pupils came in the afternoon. As Christmas approached in 1939, the majority of Moseley secondary modern pupils had been evacuated, sometimes with as little as one-day notice to pack. As for staff members, most of these joined either the Home Guard or the Fire Service, or were engaged in Anti-Aircraft duties. Shelters were erected at the school in 1940 and in that same year four bombs landed in the grounds, two of these fortunately exploding in the field, but the other two landed in the west wing and caused extensive damage to the science department. As a result, the school closed for ten days, although repairs would have to wait until the end of the war.

A few days after this raid, the school was hit again and this time incendiaries caused a blaze, which, had it not been for the swift action of one of the masters, would have taken hold in the gymnasium. The school founded a Cadet Corps and a War Savings Group as their part towards the war effort, and some 1,300 pupils served in the military, ninety-nine of whom were killed.

Local men serving in the forces were also mentioned in the national press. One of them, the Rev. Richard Newcombe, one time chaplain at Toc H. Moseley, was reported in the *Guardian* on 19 July 1940 after being awarded the Military Cross for his part in organizing the dressing and evacuation of some 300 wounded soldiers.

Three months later, on 22 October, the *Times* announced that Flying Officer Ralph Hope had been killed during air-operations. 'He was a grandson of the late Arthur

The same location on Bloomfield Road in 2007, with a post war house in its place. Note that the Gothic arch entrance to the right of this can be seen in the previous picture.

Chamberlain, cousin to Neville Chamberlain and the youngest son of Mr & Mrs Donald Hope of Moseley.'

There were many acts of heroism by local people going about their daily lives during the bombing raids and several of these were reported in the *London Gazette*.

In October 1940, Alfred Jervis, a hotel house porter who was employed at the Heathfield Hotel in Moseley, received the King's Commendation after he used a ladder to force entry into an upper floor of the building to extinguish a fire caused by a German incendiary. After this, he tackled other similar devices, which had fallen elsewhere in the neighbourhood.

That same year on the night of 26 October, Jack Reynolds, a casual labourer, came upon the scene of a direct hit by a high explosive bomb. In what had once been 163 Brighton Road, six occupants were still trapped in the cellar. Placing himself at great personal risk from falling debris and threat of structural collapse, Jack Reynolds volunteered to crawl along exposed beams to enter the cellar by way of a small hole. He rescued three injured people and one who was uninjured. After reporting that there were still two others inside whom he was not able to carry out, the rescue team passed

The Phoenix pre-fabs on Wake Green Road. These were built as emergency housing for people who had been bombed out of their homes during the Blitz and as a temporary measure, but they are still occupied here in 2008.

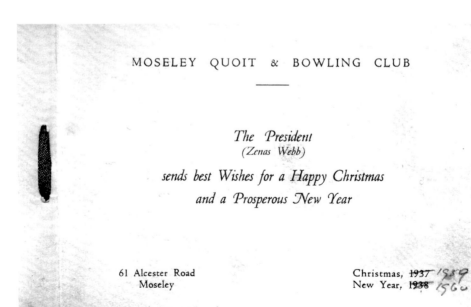

MOSELEY   QUOIT   &   BOWLING   CLUB

The President
(Zenas Webb)

*sends best Wishes for a Happy Christmas
and a Prosperous New Year*

61 Alcester Road
Moseley

Christmas, ~~1937~~ 1959
New Year, ~~1938~~ 1960

Christmas and New Year greetings from Moseley Quoit and Bowling Club, for the years 1959-60. Zenas Webb was clearly its president for some time.

Wake Green Road at the junction with Church Road on the left, *c.* 1950.

The same junction in 2008.

Located to the right of the grass on the previous picture stands Meteor Buildings (82-90), St Mary's Row. This line of shops was erected around the same time Meteor Garage (behind) opened in February 1933.

through rope and a sheet of iron, which they used to slide out the pair. For his actions, Jack Reynolds was awarded the British Empire Medal.

On 23 November 1940, Station Officer Mosedale received orders to proceed to 110 Yardley Wood Road with breathing apparatus, as there were three occupants trapped inside the damaged building. As he made his way along Showel Green Road, a high explosive bomb exploded twenty yards in front of him. He slammed on the breaks, but by the time he came to a halt some three quarters of the vehicle was hanging over the thirty-foot wide and twenty-foot deep crater, which had been opened in the middle of the road. Unable to shift the lorry due to damage to the underside and to the sump, and although being severely shaken by the blast, Officer Mosedale made his way on foot to the nearest fire station, which was in Court Road, Sparkbrook. Here, he contacted the ARP depot who put both a car and driver at his disposal so he could he continue his journey to 110 Yardley Wood Road. Arriving on the site and despite intense bombing, he, along with an ARP Rescue Squad, succeeded in extricating the occupants. For this and similar actions just over a fortnight later on 11 November in Grantham Road, Sparkhill, Officer Mosedale was awarded the George Cross (the civilians' VC).

Members of the St Mary's congregation had set up a form of advisory service to help women who, with the departure of their men folk, had found themselves alone and in need of help in coping with the everyday running of business and dealing with family matters. The Women's Volunteer Service also provided necessary aid and comfort for those affected by the bombing.

As in the First World War, a number of hostels were opened around the village, but this time it was for those who had been bombed out. One such place was 29 Chantry Road, and another was at 8 Amesbury Road. There were also prefabricated homes erected, under the Temporary Housing Act to cater for these unfortunates.

One line of these homes (Phoenix prefabs) stood on Alcester Road, near the junction of Queensbridge Road, opposite the Ambler funeral home. These were demolished some time in the early 1980s. There are, however, sixteen surviving examples on the Wake Green Road, and these are apparently the only listed prefabs in Britain.

Once the conventional German air raids had finally come to an end, there was a fresh wave of panic across the country as Hitler launched the first of his Terror Weapons in the form of robotic missiles, the V-1, better known as 'buzz bombs' or 'doodlebugs'. Launched from sites in northern France, these would fly across the channel, usually in the direction of London, above which the engine would suddenly cut-out causing the high explosive projectile to plummet down blindly, like the V-2, the world's first missile rocket. Although these never reached the Midlands they caused further waves of evacuees to the area from London and the South East.

SEVEN

The Post-War Years to the Present

Changes and Continued Resistance

So many events and changes have taken place in Moseley over the past sixty-three years that it is not easy to bring us right up to date within a single chapter covering the period since the end of the Second World War.

Village life during the four years duration of the First World War merited its own chapter, as did the twenty-one years representing the interwar years and the five and a half years covering the Second World War. The impact of this collective thirty-year period changed the lives of people worldwide, and the repercussions continue to do so. A painful example of this is the Moseley area itself. Just prior to the First World War, Moseley was considered one of the most affluent and prosperous suburbs around the city in which to live. It has been said that Moseley has become a victim of it own success, and in this there is no doubt more than a mere element of truth. How we view success depends much on how we define it. Initially, it was the countryside which was to suffer when the hamlet was transformed from rural idyll — a green lung a little over two miles from the dirt, smoke and grime of an industrial city — to a colony of those who had thrived and continued to do so from the fruits therein. Here they sought an escape. As we have seen from our little tour through time, their seclusion was indeed limited, as more and more of the working class searched for their own little stake in this suburban utopia, and as the larger, more influential families began to both die and move out, their once-exclusive properties either fell into decay, were demolished or converted into multiple dwellings, bringing a new face, or rather many new faces, to the village scene. These many changes I will deal with here in two thirty-year periods in order to do them some sort of justice.

1950s-1970s

By the middle of the 1950s, when war-time rationing had ended and the bomb sites were at last being cleared away, many immigrants from across the commonwealth began to arrive on Britain's shores; many heading for the large industrial cities where work and cheap accommodation would be available. Large numbers of these, mainly from the Indian sub-continent and the West Indies, settled in suburbs around Birmingham,

69

Slightly further down from Meteor Buildings along Wake Green Road stood another large house, of which only the front wall and stone gatepost can be seen in this 1976 picture. The land had returned to undergrowth.

like Aston, Handsworth, Nechells, Sparkbrook, Sparkhill, Balsall Heath and, of course, Moseley. Here, many of the recently-converted large houses and terraces offered relatively cheap board and lodgings close by the city. Thankfully, building in Moseley during the 1950s-1970s has not been on a large scale, although one could argue that what there has been is still too much.

Many of the changes within and around Moseley, which began in the 1950-1960s, were probably brought about more as a result of changing population than development, although it seemed that by the 1960s everywhere was undergoing change, including people. Moseley became something of a magnet, if not a little later, the 'Midlands Mecca' for many of the youths of the counter-culture and dispossessed of society. It doubtless followed that drugs were to become a big problem in the area, with so many from diverse backgrounds and locations being thrown together as neighbours.

Many students too came to Moseley in search of bedsits that were not too far from the Birmingham universities. Other settlers to the area were those receiving treatment for mental illness at the local clinics and hospitals. It takes no great feat of imagination to visualise many of the bizarre occurrences that were to arise from this perilous concoction during the following decade. Prostitution too had become a problem, as it

By the 1980s, a pensioner's village had risen on the site (see previous photo), pictured here in 2008.

already had been in Balsall Heath for quite some time. By the early 1960s, it had spilt over into Moseley and various residents' committees had been set up in an attempt to address the issue. The crisis was exacerbated in 1967 when a major red-light area in Balsall Heath was demolished. Many of the prostitutes there had rented out rooms for £11 a day (a lot of money then), with another girl renting the room at the same rate for night-shift! Now the prostitutes were coming to Moseley in search of cheap rooms (and finding them) from which to operate. Meanwhile, the secretary of the Anderton Park Road Residents' Association had caused uproar by suggesting that the corporation should have a purpose-built tenement of single rooms built (but not in Moseley), which could be supervised by the police and health authorities — similar to those in Hamburg. The problem was to remain in the area for many years to come and during that time various measures were taken by the residents and local groups. These included taking the registration numbers of known kerb-crawlers, picketing the corners where the prostitutes stood and the use of stickers placed on offending vehicles. Further, more extreme measures were carried out by vigilantes, and kerb-crawlers were ambushed and pelted with stones as they cruised around the village streets, many leaving with no windows intact!

By the 1970s, many of the old houses in the area were suffering as a result of under capitalised private landlords. These were failing, or unwilling, to keep up with repairs or maintenance in the dark economic climate which prevailed at that time, which resulted in the demolition of quite a few such buildings. Others were spared and bought by housing organisations who completely gutted and refurbished them, turning them into multiple, self-contained flats rather than bed-sits. Despite all these problems it is a curious fact that Moseley experienced something of a cultural boom during those difficult years, and this in spite of or as a result of the same explosive mix within the community as has been described earlier. So many gifted individuals were pursuing their own various artistic fields within such confined proximity and gelling together to form writers, poets and theatrical groups, artist's co-operatives and, of course, musicians were always putting bands together. All were encouraged to take advantage of the many venues available to them around the village in which to exhibit or perform. Local bands played in the upstairs room above the Fighting Cocks and the Trafalgar. There were poetry readings and art exhibitions held at various venues including the art gallery at the top of Salisbury Road and at Woodbridge House, as well as co-operative premises. The homes of private individuals were used to establish the *Moseley Paper* and *Moseley Arts Paper*, both of which reported current affairs of local interest as well as advertising and reviewing the diverse cultural events taking place, many of which reached their peak in this era. Moseley at this time had quite a reputation throughout the Midlands for its Bohemian atmosphere and somewhat eccentric inhabitants and many travelled to the area out of curiosity, to see if for themselves.

One local, Harry Nicholas, was moved to write in the *Moseley Paper* during that time:

> Living here is like stepping into a painting by Breughel, in modern dress. Here are the scholars, drunkards, religious people, musicians, prostitutes, writers, happy people and sad. Some incredibly sad people, actors, painters, professionals and derelicts, every class and type... It might well be a fools head, but I wonder whether the feeling that is Moseley has always been here, bringing the village to itself; or whether it is the village's presence which creates and sustains the feeling... the feeling is strong enough to hold together all the diverse facets into an eccentric family and community; like you, and me, and him and her.

In his reasoning, Mr Nicholas was certainly not alone as there were many others who were to express similar sentiments, and some even maintaining that Moseley village stood on some long-lost ley line!

In keeping with this character, there were, scattered around the village, small co-operatives, workshops, makeshift temples, self-help and community support groups. On the Ladypool Road there was the Lane neighbourhood advice centre, and if you couldn't get the help you needed there then there was the Scientology centre on St Mary's Row, where passers by were frequently stopped by devotees, armed with pen and clipboard, offering free personality tests. There was at least one whole food shop and an 'alternative' or some may say 'underground' shop known as Prometheus at 134 Alcester Road, which sold a wide variety of books on politics, psychology, philosophy, sociology, the arts, yoga, meditation, mysticism, sex, drugs and so forth. Downstairs in

This large house on the south side of Forest Road was later converted into quarters for nurses working at Sorrento (behind on Wake Green Road). They are seen here in the process of demolition in July 1981.

the cellar was Ben-eatheus (a real underground shop!) which, when it opened on 12 June 1976, was described by the *Moseley Paper* as being in 'what feels like an ancient cave'. Down here were all manner of things of interest to many in the local community. There were kaftans, brightly coloured Moroccan embroidered clothing, handmade jewellery, perfumes, incense and incense burners, oriental ornaments, as well as a wide variety of wood and soapstone ware, including some very exotic smoking apparatus.

Mention must also be made of the well-known low-budget café called the Gigi, for many years at 32 St Mary's Row. It was named after the 1958 film and run by a lovable old cockney Jewess, Hilda Bloomfield, who was always on hand with a sympathetic ear or words of advice for her many patrons in need. It was a popular meeting place for the locals and a drop-in centre for many of those receiving treatment for mental illness. Hilda managed the Gigi for quite a number of years with help from one or two of her friends. Even though it was a very popular venue and sometimes open after pub closing time, she eventually had to let it go and move out to Five-Ways. A short tribute to her was printed in *Birmingham 13*, which acknowledged the fine service she had provided for the community, calling her an unsung heroine and wishing her 'a belated bouquet for her quiet good works'.

Moseley Festivals

This was the decade of the early Moseley Festivals, the first Community Arts Festival being in June 1975. There was, as I remember, a very busy atmosphere about the village, with forty different events taking place at various venues, like the Jazz Night and Old-Time Music Hall. There was at least one Shakespearian performance by a local theatrical group and a barbeque. All these sponsored events helped raise money for a number of different charities during the festival. Needless to say, the local pubs entered into the spirit of the occasion and benefited as a result of the increased activity that was

Ashwood Court on Forest Road now stands where the nurse's quarters were, pictured here in 2007.

generated. None perhaps more so than the Fighting Cocks, which exhibited paintings by local artists and leased out the upstairs room for some of the events. Ivor Bartlett was the publican at the time and the following year took part here in a public debate with John Luker, the old established village baker, and others on the subject 'The Festival and the Nature of Community Life in Moseley'.

The population of Moseley at this time was estimated at around 15,000, at least 7,000 of whom took part in the festival activities. The festival of 1976 was a bigger and better organised affair; one of the many features included a Beatles and Stones disco, and even an evening of music from Germany's Weimar years! Another team competition was the Moseley Mastermind Quiz as a challenge for the many intellectuals of the village. Another year a 'village idiot' was nominated and he was required to perform certain tasks, one of which was to set up a table and chair and eat a meal in the middle of the road at the junction. Needless to say, this activity was interrupted by the local police.

The festivals were organised by various teams, which seemed to change yearly as some left and others joined, but all apparently suffered through lack of cash and support. Sometimes the festival ran at a loss, like that of 1978 when there were eighty-four events and the Folk concert finished £150 down. However, once established, everyone seemed to take it for granted that another festival would be arranged, and they generally were. The high point of the festival was often considered to be the street procession. These usually took place on a Saturday morning and all the various organizations involved had a decorative float created and the High Street was lined with bunting and stalls selling all sorts, including locally-produced craft wares. Amongst the many local beneficiaries of the Moseley Festival was our own Sorrento Maternity Hospital, which had been ear-marked for closure in the 1970s. The campaign to keep it open was long and sustained and during this time the hospital continued to provide a first-class service. Much funding was provided by the generosity of the local community, which helped to buy expensive life-saving equipment. There was a sponsored 'bed-push' which took the form of a procession of nurses and other supporters marching voluntary 'patients' along the village High Street to King' Heath and back again, via Ladypool Road. The League of Friends had donated £1,500 to Sorrento towards a foetal heart monitor and the 'bed-push' raised the extra £2,000 needed. This was so successful that another such drive was arranged shortly afterwards to raise another £1,500 for an arterial oxygen monitor to be installed in the Special Care Unit.

In 1978, Dr Nichol, the Area Medical Officer, branded the Sorrento 'an obstetrical slum'! Calling for its closure, he added, 'Children in this day and age should not be born in such conditions that exist at Sorrento.' This view was certainly at odds with the many dedicated staff who worked there and countless mothers across the region that had given birth at Sorrento. This statement was blasted in the *Moseley Paper*, which ran a long campaign of support for the hospital, with the claim that Dr Nichols had never even visited Sorrento and the outrageous statement was in fact based upon the outdated report of an engineer.

Fresh hope for the hospital came when the Area Health Authority began investing more money for improvements to the site and the building was renovated in 1979. Whilst the work was in progress, patients and staff were temporarily moved out to Selly Oak Hospital and it seemed that this move had granted at least a ten-year stay of execution for Sorrento. Its contribution to the health service at this time may be better

The first Moseley Festival was held in 1975 and although they were usually struggling affairs, they were enjoyed by many. The badges became coveted collectable items.

appreciated when one considers that Selly Oak Hospital accounted for 1,000 births a year, whilst Sorrento's 'output' was double that at 2,000.

Other campaigns being fought by the villagers in the form of the Moseley Tenants Association and other bodies, was the City Development Plan, which threatened the area and a bypass proposal. A further instrument in the village arsenal was to be the Moseley Society, which was established in 1979. One of its aims is the protection and preservation of the historic aspects of the area and at the same time to promote high standards of modern architecture, where it is deemed necessary, which is at least in keeping with the earlier buildings thereabout. The Moseley Society is a chief organiser of meetings, which are held to address issues of public interest and serves on local advisory bodies. Amongst its many achievements, it can claim success in opposing the proposed road widening at the crossroads, opposition to the M40 link, the restoration of the Dovecote, the ice house, support for the two Moseley conservation areas, the Forum of Moseley Community Development Trust and the formation of the Local History Society.

Villagers on the green during the festival of 1978.

Left: Local musician Steve Ajao with his band The Wide Boys playing at the village green during the 1978 Moseley Festival.

Below: Not such strange goings on taking place on 'Bog Island', 1978.

In 1979, the Moseley Festival ran from 15-24 June. However, it was a struggling event, which, by all accounts, cost more to run than it raised. The ever-popular street procession that year included the yet to be discovered band UB40, who later played at the Arena in Cannon Hill Park.

1980s-90s

In 1980, a new team was formed to organise the festival, headed as chairman by Dave Cox the butcher. This was only a three-day affair, but it was well arranged and ran smoothly. The year 1981 followed a similar pattern and saw the start of the nine-mile Moseley Marathon, which was to become a more or less ongoing feature of the festivals to come. UB40, by now a successful band, performed a free gig once more at the Arena, which was packed to capacity. Highly collectable and eagerly anticipated were the commemorative Moseley Festival badges, which appeared each year to mark the occasion. However, in 1982, they seemed to have been overlooked, so I designed and produced one of these retrospectively to fill the gap for collectors. I made them available the following year along with the current issue, and continued to design and produce them until 1987. By this time, circumstances had taken me outside the village and I didn't get to many of the festivals after that year. It appears that no one took over from me, and as far as I know the tradition has been discontinued.

Perhaps the most positive development of this decade was the designation on 17 March 1983 of the Moseley Conservation Area. This encompassed the village centre and several streets surrounding it to an area of 52.81 hectares, including some 1,083 residential properties. The character appraisal of the Moseley Conservation Area and associated Management Plan was prepared with the help of the Moseley Society in accord with English Heritage guidelines, and it is a welcome safeguard against further wanton destruction or alteration to buildings of historic architectural importance and unsympathetic building and development that is detrimental to the character of the village. There have been to date two other extensions to Moseley Conservation Area, one on 12 November 1987 and the last one on 14 March 2005, bringing the total of 95.06 hectares (234.92 acres) within its boundary. The area around St Agnes' church is a secondary conservation area, and there are proposals to extend these borders in the future.

Despite this ray of light, the latter part of the 1980s and early 1990s was attended by something of a gloomy atmosphere. During that time, a somewhat dark cloud hung over the village. The High Street became very untidy and there were many empty premises, their doors and windows covered over by bill stickers, wooden boarding and graffiti. There were problems with litter, street drinkers and beggars and the annual festivals, which nearly did not happen, were unable to do anything to alleviate the gloom. On the contrary, they too suffered under the climate of decay. The usual factors seem to plague the co-ordination and running of this event: lack of input, enthusiasm and participation. So bleak was it, that by 1991 it seemed that the festival was indeed going to die a death. However, it hung on until 1993, when a new festival committee was formed. With a lot of effort, it managed to kick-start new life into the event, and even managed to raise £2,000 for charity. Over the next four years, things continued to improve and it showed in the quality of events, the festival funds and, happily, the general mood in the village.

Left: Sponsored 'bed-push' at Moseley Festival to raise money for Sorrento Maternity Hospital in 1981.

Below: St Mary's Row in 1986. The Gigi café, something of a local drop-in (or drop-out) centre, can be seen to the left of Pottery & Pieces.

In 1993, the closure of the Gracewell Clinic, a residential unit for sex-offenders that had been in operation for five years — against local approval — was the successful conclusion of another long-fought campaign in the village.

Unwittingly, Moseley found itself at the centre of another campaign a couple of years later. On Saturday 5 August 1995, there was serious disruption on the high street, which had been closed to traffic by hoards of banner-wielding demonstrators proclaiming, 'Reclaim the Streets!' A police van and several police motorcycles were nearby and there were police officers diverting the traffic and buses up the otherwise unfamiliar route of Woodbridge Road. On the high street, a band played loud music through huge speakers from the back of a lorry, whilst a variety of performers entertained the somewhat bemused crowds that had gathered. What seemed to many to be something of an impromptu affair, obviously had some form of organisation behind it, but who and what was it all about? Nobody seemed to know. Reclaim the streets — was it something to do with the growing problem of traffic congestion on the high street, an ongoing issue of great concern to local people over the past few years?

As it transpired, the whole event was orchestrated by a group called Road Alert, which was based in Newbury. There they had demonstrated against their own bypass, as well as the M11 link road in London, the A30 in Devon, Wells and Manchester. This group also provided training for treetop protesters and had a local contact group in the Moseley area. The village, it seems, had been Road Alert's venue of choice. They were doubtless aware of the strong stand taken by the villagers in opposition to various other road-building schemes, including the M42 feed road that had threatened the area and which had been successfully defeated. Whilst Kwiksave felt the pinch on this day, some of the smaller shops did quite a roaring trade in providing food and refreshments to the gathered throngs.

Moseley in the Millennium

A further campaign spilt over from the end of the twentieth century. It was known as the 'no more pubs' crusade, which began when Bass Taverns, who had opened O'Neil's opposite the supermarket on Alcester Road, were intent on annexing the vacant property next door to expand their business. Opposition prevented them from doing this, but it was to be only one battle in an ongoing war. The next round went to the Wetherspoon's chain who, despite opposition, succeeded in opening a branch on St Mary's Row in 2006, known as the Elizabeth of York. At least there was a local connection with this name, as she was the patroness who gave land in the sixteenth century for the building of the parish church. This sentiment did little to appease the protesters campaigning against yet more drinking establishments in the village, and by 2007, Moseley was declared a Saturation Area under the 2003 Licensing Act, which was empowered to block applications for new drinking premises.

'Time Has Been Called in Moseley — the Birmingham Suburb with a Bohemian Reputation' proclaimed the *Birmingham Post* on 13 November 2007. It went on to announce the decision made by the City Council Cabinet to enforce the Act following protests co-ordinated by resident groups, the local Community Association, the police and the Moseley Society, highlighting the fact that there were already ten pubs and

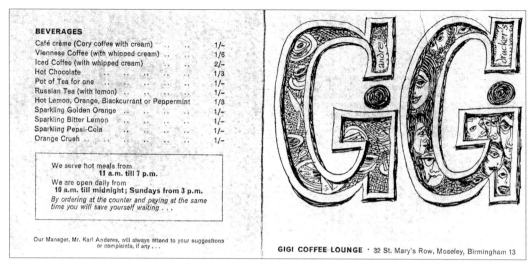

BEVERAGES

Café crème (Cory coffee with cream)	1/–
Viennese Coffee (with whipped cream)	1/6
Iced Coffee (with whipped cream)	2/–
Hot Chocolate	1/3
Pot of Tea for one	1/–
Russian Tea (with lemon)	1/–
Hot Lemon, Orange, Blackcurrant or Peppermint	1/3
Sparkling Golden Orange	1/–
Sparkling Bitter Lemon	1/–
Sparkling Pepsi-Cola	1/–
Orange Crush	1/–

We serve hot meals from
11 a.m. till 7 p.m.
We are open daily from
10 a.m. till midnight; Sundays from 3 p.m.
By ordering at the counter and paying at the same time you will save yourself waiting . . .

Our Manager, Mr. Karl Anderes, will always attend to your suggestions or complaints, if any . . .

GIGI COFFEE LOUNGE · 32 St. Mary's Row, Moseley, Birmingham 13

A menu from Gigi Coffee lounge, 32 St Mary's Row, Moseley. It dates to the 1960s.

SOUP OF THE DAY 1/–

CONTINENTAL SPECIALITIES

Viennese Gulash (Paprika Beef Stew)	4/6
Stuffed Paprika (sweet Hungarian pepper stuffed with minced meat and rice)	3/6 & 5/6
Polish Meatballs (minced pork)	3/6
Stuffed Vine Leaves	4/–
Veal or Pork Cotelet in mushroom sauce	6/6
Choice of rice or potatoes with these meals	
Frankfurters with Sauerkraut or pickled vegetables	4/–
Spaghetti with meat sauce	3/–
Vol-au-vent (savoury)	2/6

OMELETTES

Plain Omelette, with bread and butter	3/–
Ham	4/–
Cheese	4/–
Mushroom	4/–
Two Pancakes, with jam or lemon	1/9

They are all made to order, so there is some waiting time

SNACKS ON TOAST

Egg	1/9
Spaghetti	1/9
Cheese	1/9
Beans	1/9
Beefburger	1/6
An extra round of toast	6d.

SANDWICHES, freshly made

Ham	full round	1/6
Cheese	full round	1/6
Egg	full round	1/6
Buttered Toast	full round	6d.

CONTINENTAL GATEAUX, CAKES, etc.
are supplied by Drucker's VIENNA Patisserie and baked daily fresh at own bakery fresh whipped cream .. per portion 6d.

MRS. TATAR'S SPECIALS:

Home-made Stuffed Cabbage	3/6
Meat Loaf, Creamed Potatoes, Peas	4/–
Chicken Paprikas (one day notice)	7/6

Reverse of the menu.

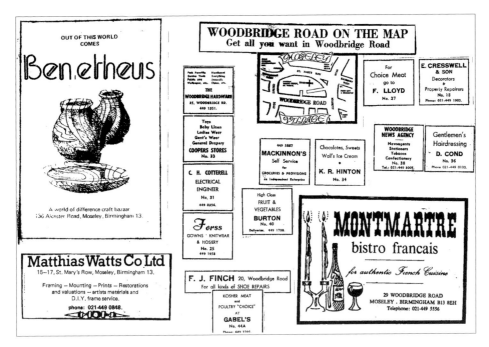

Advert.

This old house, pictured in 1992 shortly before demolition, once stood on the corner of Woodstock and Woodhurst Roads.

Above and below: Part of a row of old terrace houses that stood on the left-hand side of Trafalgar Road (Woodbridge behind you) and were allowed to fall into disrepair. Seen here in August 1992, shortly before demolition.

At the rear of what is presently O'Neil's public house on Alcester Road, once stood the premises of the old Moseley Mews Cab Company, part of which is seen here the day before it was demolished in 1997.

Tornado damage. On the afternoon of 28 July 2005, a violent tornado tore through the village and, although people were injured, there were, fortunately, no fatalities. However, much damage was done to trees and properties. Here, a large tree has fallen from the front garden of 57 Anderton Park Road, crumbling the wall and blocking the roadway.

Further up at the corner of Anderton Park and Forest Roads, the tornado caused expensive damage to rare and ornate Italianate roofing-tiles. Fortunately, these have since been accurately restored.

Above: A collapsed chimney stack and damaged roof tiles on a property on Sandford Road, pictured the day after the tornado.

Right: Three months after the tornado that did so much damage to old properties in Moseley in 2005, bungling developers added to the toll by demolishing numbers 16-18 St Mary's Row, which were protected buildings within the conservation area. They were subsequently made to rebuild the façade using the same materials.

Despite the efforts of the Moseley Society and locals interested in preserving the fine old houses of the village, wanton neglect still persists. This stretch of properties (124-130) at the top of Anderton Park Road were once connected to Sorrento Hospital and, as can be seen by this picture taken in 2007, they have been left empty for many years, boarded up and criminally allowed to fall into disrepair by their owner.

The John Murray Buildings, St Mary's Row in 2007, still standing despite many changes. Traces of the "Upton's Provisions Warehouse" sign can still be seen level with the builders plaque.

Above: Wetherspoon's opened the Elizabeth of York on St Mary's Row in 2006 despite local opposition to the number of public houses in the area.

Right: The Farmers' Market has been a regular feature in Moseley since 1999, although it was temporarily interrupted in 2002 due to Foot and Mouth Disease. This picture, by Brett Wilde, was taken *c.* 2006.

One of the surviving old Birmingham Corporation lampposts stands on Ascot Road in 2007. These were replaced at the end of the 1970s and have for the most part disappeared.

An old ceramic cream jar of Cold Bath Farm.

six licensed restaurants within half a mile in the area. The chief concerns were crime, drunkenness, noise and traffic congestion, especially at night time.

Tornado

Undoubtedly the most devastating singular incident to affect Moseley in recent time has to be the violent tornado that tore through south Birmingham suburbs at around 2.30 BST on the afternoon of 28 July 2005. It wreaked havoc and devastation in its course through Small Heath, Sparkbrook, Balsall Heath, Moseley and King's Heath. Hundreds of buildings were damaged, many irreparably, and hundreds of trees were uprooted and felled, crushing vehicles and blocking roads. Miraculously, no one was killed although there were a number of injuries sustained.

The tornado, which had a general T4 rating on the TORRO scale, was one of the strongest recorded in the United Kingdom for thirty years with winds between 93-130 miles per hour. In the Moseley area, Ladypool Road took the brunt and the place resembled a war zone as the Emergency Services quickly responded. The Fire Service received more than 240 calls for help within the first hour, and twenty-five fire engines, along with one hundred personnel, were deployed to conduct searches of collapsed buildings, looking for people trapped in the ruins. Fortunately, there were none, but the damage sustained was enormous. An estimated 1,000 trees were toppled and damages caused set at around £40 million — the costliest tornado in British records.

As if enough damages to many of Moseley's old buildings had not already been done, just three months after the tornado, on 7 November 2005, bungling contractors demolished numbers 16-18 St Mary's Row, despite it being a protected building within the conservation area. The vandals, Off The Wall Properties, tore down the frontage and floors of the two terraced-buildings that had formed part of what was Birmingham's only surviving Edwardian shopping precinct. The City Council, seeking to prosecute the felons, ordered the developers to rebuild the property brick by brick, using all the original materials. This has now been completed. Councillor Martin Mullaney remarked, 'We hope this will send a message to other developers that you don't just demolish buildings willy-nilly.'

600th Anniversary

The year 2005 also saw the 600th anniversary of St Mary's Parish and the re-location of Moseley Rugby Club to its new grounds on Billesley Common, after being removed from the Reddings to Bournbrook at the end of the 1999-2000 seasons. Moseley Rugby Club, in its distinctive red and black colours, first played at the Reddings in 1880 when they defeated Leicester. Here they went from strength to strength defeating many other opponents, including the first-ever tourists, The Moaris in 1888. The success of Moseley and the name the Reddings was kept foremost in the minds and headlines of the rugby world by the club since that time. Sadly, during the 1990s, it ran into financial difficulties and went into administration early in 1998, and the Reddings was subject

An unsympathetic but very imaginative blend of the past and present is brought together in this picture by local photographer Brett Wilde.

Birmingham looms in the distance. This picture was taken by Brett Wilde from the top of Queensbridge Road School *c.* 2006.

of a delayed sale to Bryant Homes, making the future of the club uncertain. By 2000, it was out of administration and, although financial problems continued to persist, the club is now fighting back from its new grounds.

In May 2008, the Jug of Ale, formerly Gilligans and originally the Prince Regent, finally closed its doors after being one of Birmingham's best-known music venues for bands like Oasis, Ocean Colour Scene and many others over the past sixteen years. Rumours about development of the site drift between conversion into an Indian restaurant, conversion/demolition for a block of flats and to demolition of the building for another supermarket.

Having now come up to date, I can find little else to say concerning the village and its past, at least for the present. What lies ahead we shall have to wait and see. In the meantime, it is always a good and rewarding, if somewhat sobering, experience to look back once in awhile, giving reflection on all that has gone before, as we go about our often all-too-busy lives.

The tendency to reminisce and the love of nostalgia — inherent qualities peculiar to humans — have long been present within us, and, as in the case of the village folk, change has long been seen as something to resist and bygone time often the yardstick by which we measure our preferences and ideals for the present day. It is, perhaps, fitting for me to bring this book to a close using the sentiments penned 114 years ago by a writer of the *Moseley Society Journal* in November 1894, who said, regarding the history of the village until then, that the most remarkable fact was the rapidity with which the hamlet became a suburb of Birmingham. Between the village and the big city was, but a few generations ago, some two and a half miles of pleasant pasture, meadow and hilly fields, which likewise stretched on after it, continuing through Kings Heath and onwards. A narrow plank spanned the Rea, where lobsters and all sorts of fish may be found and the population of Balsall Heath dwelt in half a dozen large houses and a couple of cottages. The journeyman arriving in the village would find there the old timber framed houses, which had nestled around the roadway for several hundred years. He might be familiar with the site of the local squires on horseback riding by and traders with their carts going about their daily business, as if time itself were non-existent. There was laughter from the local inns and the ringing of the blacksmith's hammer as he beat out his living in the premises behind. There was sometimes a crackling fire on the village green, where oxen was roast in those far-away times, when the Taylor's occupied the old hall, the Anderton's the big mansion on Belle Walk and the Holder's at Moor Green, long before Highbury or Uffculme were built in Yew-tree fields.

With all of this in mind, and somewhat resignedly, the writer, then some seventeen years before annexation with the city, concluded by saying:

> The time is not far distant when Moseley will be absorbed in Birmingham, and then the history of the district may be fully written: it will form by no means the least interesting portion of the annals of the midland metropolis.

Further Reading

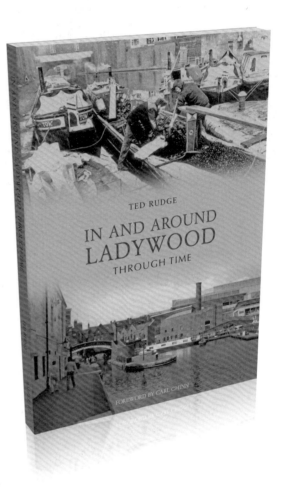

*In and Around Ladywood
Through Time*
Ted Rudge

Paperback | 235 x 165mm
96 pages and 180 full colour
images

ISBN 978-1-84868-569-7
£12.99

Available from all good bookshops, or order direct
from our website www.amberleybooks.com